REA

FRIENDS
OF ACPL

P9-AOF-562

DEC 0 1 2007

Praise for Abraham J. Twerski's Work

"Provides us with an understanding of our spiritual side.... It's like a conversation with a warm and trusted friend."
—**Betty Ford,** former first lady; founder, Betty Ford Treatment Center

"Written with clarity, compassion, comics and practical wisdom ... harvests a lifetime of spiritual study, psychological counseling and life experience guiding us to be our best and our happiest."
—**Rabbi Elie Kaplan Spitz,** author, *Does the Soul Survive? A Jewish Journey to Belief in Afterlife, Past Lives & Living with Purpose*

"Reveals that there can never be true happiness without spirituality. The essence of true happiness is in realizing oneself and being the best human being one can be—and that is spirituality."
—**Christopher Kennedy Lawford,** author, *Symptoms of Withdrawal: A Memoir of Snapshots and Redemption*

"Much more than studying genetic factors, set points, or diet prescriptions, Dr. Twerski's simple examples and entertaining explanations make reading this book a happy and life changing event."
—**Judi Hollis, PhD,** author, *Hot & Heavy: Finding Your Soul through Food and Sex* and *From Bagels to Buddha*

"I defy anyone to read this book and not become kinder, more spiritual and insightful. For people of all faiths, and of none, by one of the great Jewish teachers of our age. If you want to be a blessing in the lives of those around you, and in your own life, read this book."
—**Rabbi Joseph Telushkin,** author, *A Code of Jewish Ethics* and *Jewish Literacy*

"[A] careful delineation of Spiritual Deficiency Syndrome and a detailed presentation of the aspects of the unique human spirit will smooth the path for undertaking ten steps to happiness. Gentle humor and subtle stories will weave their way into your life. This appreciation of spirituality will make anyone want to pursue that goal ... and learn how better to do so."
—**Ernest Kurtz, PhD,** coauthor, *The Spirituality of Imperfection: Storytelling and the Search for Meaning*

"Exceptionally well-written, thought-provoking ... discusses the need in all of us to lead meaningful lives."
—**Robert J. Ackerman, PhD,** author, *A Husband's Little Black Book: Commonsense, Wit and Wisdom for a Better Marriage;* and *A Wife's Little Red Book: Commonsense, Wit and Wisdom for a Better Marriage*

"Wonderful ... explains what we are missing and how to achieve it. Filled with stories and written in a direct, personal way ... could well help people to find nothing short of meaning and happiness."

—**Elliot N. Dorff, PhD,** author,
The Way Into Tikkun Olam *(Repairing the World)*

"Brilliant.... Shows how happiness and spirituality are intertwined and achievable. Simply reading this joyful writing will put you on the road to happiness."

—**Rabbi Berel Wein,** founder and director of
The Destiny Foundation; author, *Triumph of Survival*

HAPPINESS
and the
Human Spirit

HAPPINESS
and the
Human Spirit
The Spirituality of Becoming the Best You Can Be

ABRAHAM J. TWERSKI, MD

For People of All Faiths, All Backgrounds
JEWISH LIGHTS Publishing
Woodstock, Vermont

Happiness and the Human Spirit:
The Spirituality of Becoming the Best You Can Be

2007 First Printing
© 2007 by Abraham J. Twerski

Library of Congress Cataloging-in-Publication Data

Twerski, Abraham J.
  Happiness and the human spirit: the spirituality of becoming the best you can be / Abraham J. Twerski.
      p. cm.
  Includes bibliographical references.
  ISBN-13: 978-1-58023-343-9 (hardcover)
  ISBN-10: 1-58023-343-0 (hardcover)
  1. Happiness—Religious aspects. 2. Self-actualization (Psychology)—Religious aspects. I. Title.
  BL65.H3T84 2007
  170'.44—dc22

2007027289

10 9 8 7 6 5 4 3 2 1

All the stories in this book are based on actual experiences. The names and details have been changed to protect the privacy of the people involved.

Manufactured in the United States of America
❀ Printed on recycled paper.
Jacket art and design: Melanie Robinson

For People of All Faiths, All Backgrounds
Published by Jewish Lights Publishing
A Division of Longhill Partners, Inc.
Sunset Farm Offices, Route 4, P.O. Box 237
Woodstock, VT 05091
Tel: (802) 457-4000   Fax: (802) 457-4004
www.jewishlights.com

Dedicated to all the wonderful people
who have allowed me to share their lives.

Contents

Introduction

Have you ever heard anyone say, "More happiness? Thanks any-way, but I just don't need any more. I'm as happy as I can be"? We might hear expressions such as "I've never been so happy" or "I couldn't be happier," but I doubt anyone would turn down *more* happiness. I dare say none of us has as much happiness as we would like.

Have you ever felt that you just can't quite put your finger on the reason why you're not happier? Although there are certainly some who experience severe mood disorders, such as clinical depression, that can be diagnosed and treated, more often people are bothered by a vague feeling of discontent, a persistent feeling that "something's missing."

Some people think that if only they had everything they wanted, they would be content. Others, however, do not lack anything in particular but are still discontent. It is possible that they are lacking something of which they are unaware. They may indeed have all the desires they can hear, see, touch, smell, and taste, but there is something that is not accessible to the five senses yet is an integral part of a human being, without which a person is not whole: *spirituality.*

The human spirit requires essential nutrients. To the extent that we supply these nutrients, we are happy. To the extent that we are deprived of these nutrients, we suffer from what I call Spiritual Deficiency Syndrome (SDS).

Within the pages of *Happiness and the Human Spirit*, I will explore not only what these essential nutrients are, but also how they hold the key to happiness. In essence, my point is that, to be truly happy, we need to live as spiritual beings.

I'm not talking about being religious. Although I draw on my background as a psychiatrist and a rabbi, as well as the tradition of Jewish wisdom, what I offer is for people of all faith traditions. I propose that every person can be spiritual, regardless of the degree or even presence of formal religion, by being the best person he or she can be.

If your goal is to be a happier person, I invite you to join me on this exploration of the spiritual path to happiness. I do not offer instant answers or the solutions to all your problems. Instead, I will help you look at what gives you identity as a human being and how you can exercise your human qualities to the fullest to achieve happiness as a result of living as a spiritual being. That is the path to true contentment, to a successful pursuit of happiness.

Part 1

LIFE, LIBERTY, and the PURSUIT of HAPPINESS

1

The Pursuit of Happiness

S ince time immemorial, we humans have been engaged in the pursuit of happiness. The authors of the Declaration of Independence even declared happiness to be one of our "unalienable rights." The actual achievement of happiness, however, has always been elusive. Many of us settle for freedom from discontent.

I once noticed the logo on a can of evaporated milk claiming it was "milk from contented cows." Why should we care whether the cows are content or not? Obviously, the manufacturer wants to convince us that the finest quality milk comes from the best cows, and that the best cows are contented cows. In other words, that the degree of contentment is the measurement of "cow excellence."

As desirable as contentment might be, however, it does not constitute happiness. Absence of a negative feeling does not constitute a positive feeling. Contentment is not the same as happiness, at least not *human* happiness. While being free of discontent may be fine for a cow, it does not suffice for a human being. The pursuit of happiness for us is more than that.

Where's the Happiness?

I was once invited to give a talk on "Can There Be Happiness in the Twenty-First Century?" It occurred to me that perhaps, one hundred years ago, there might have been a lecture titled, "*Will* There Be Happiness in the Twenty-First Century?" In the early days of modern medicine, science, and technology, many were hopeful that we could reach happiness through human ingenuity.

I remember, as a child, that our home was quarantined on several occasions when I had measles, chicken pox, scarlet fever, mumps, and whooping cough. Placards affixed to homes warned people of the contagious diseases within. In summer, any muscle ache raised the fear of polio. I recall the grief of a family when their seventeen-year-old daughter died of pneumonia. Every major city in the United States once had a tuberculosis sanitarium, and this disease took the lives of people in their prime. These scenarios have all but disappeared in this era of modern medicine.

Communication back then was difficult. The trip from Chicago to Los Angeles took sixty hours. While correspondence by mail was much faster than by pony express, it took at least a week to get a response to a letter. Costs of long-distance calls were prohibitive. Two-way wireless communication existed only in the fantasy world of comic strips, in Dick Tracy's two-way wrist radio. But even fantasy could not imagine sending text messages or watching a football game on a hand-held telephone. And readers of the Buck Rogers cartoon strip certainly gave no serious thought to space travel.

During the first half of the twentieth century, earning a livelihood required long hours and often much physical labor, and the workplace was usually not a pleasant place. There were no instant foods, no microwaves, and few fast-food restaurants. On torrid days there was little relief from sweltering heat. (I recall the first appearance of air-conditioning: it was in theaters. The only relief we could find on a hot day was to stay in the theater for a double feature.)

For anyone in the early 1900s, the vision that crippling polio would be eliminated; that the contagious diseases of childhood would be a rarity; that the trip from Chicago to Los Angeles would be a trip of *four* rather than sixty hours; that the Atlantic Ocean could be traversed in seven hours; that, on the hottest days of summer, we could relax in the comfort of air-conditioned homes, watching a football game being played three thousand miles away, or a choice of movies on DVD—that would be paradise on Earth!

If you could tell such a person that, in the twenty-first century, the workweek would be thirty-seven hours; that most of the work would be done by electronically controlled machines; that preparation of meals would be facilitated by the availability of instant foods, microwaves, and fast-food vendors; that fax machines, cell phones, and e-mail would enable instant communication; that humans would orbit the Earth and walk on the moon; that computers would make the most complex calculations in a fraction of a second and predict the weather with great accuracy; that diseased livers and kidneys would be replaced by healthy organs; that the Internet would put all the knowledge in the world at our fingertips—they would see such a future as pure bliss! Surely, with so many of the sources of distress and suffering eliminated, the human race would finally be able to achieve the goal of happiness. The pursuit would be over!

So here we are, in the twenty-first century, the beneficiaries of heretofore unimaginable miracles of science and technology, yet happiness continues to elude us. Furthermore, it is difficult to imagine what science and technology can do that will result in happiness. Will we really be happier if we send someone to Mars? Will we really be happier if we acquire the technological marvel of a television set that can be suspended from the showerhead so we can watch TV while showering? Can it be that happiness will still elude our grasp?

We have so much, yet we have so little!

Happiness Hide-and-Seek

It has become abundantly clear that science and technology have given us undreamed-of conveniences—but not happiness. There is simply nothing that is guaranteed to bring happiness. Yet, we relentlessly pursue happiness. Shall we conclude that this happiness is a delusion beyond our reach? Is it possible that every human being has a drive that is doomed to frustration? Or, perhaps, is it just that we have been searching for happiness in the wrong places?

Some have sought the answer in psychology and psychiatry. We have unprecedented psychiatric medications, and we can often cure severe depressions and other disabling symptoms. But while we may be able to successfully treat people to bring them out of a depression, psychiatry and psychology cannot deliver happiness. Happiness is not merely the absence of misery.

Many have looked for happiness in religion. Yet, if any of the world's great religions had been able to provide its adherents with happiness, its secret would have surfaced eventually, and everyone in pursuit of happiness would have created a torrent in their rush to join.

You may be familiar with the story of a peasant in a tiny village in Poland who had a repetitive dream that, at the base of a bridge in Prague, a huge treasure was buried. Not being able to free himself of this thought, he made the grueling trip to Prague. Alas, there were always police around the bridge, and he could not dig for the treasure.

One of the police noticed this peasant, who was hoping for a moment when there would be no police present. "Why are you hanging around here?" the policeman asked. The peasant told him of his dream.

The policeman howled with laughter. "So, because of this dream you came all the way here? Why, I have had a repetitive dream that under the floor of a peasant's hut in a tiny village in Poland there lies buried a huge treasure. Do you think I am so foolish as to travel there to find it?"

The peasant returned home, lifted up the floorboards, and found the treasure.

Within the context of this book, the moral of the story may become obvious: the treasure of happiness cannot be found outside of ourselves; it lies within us. But too often we are unaware of it. We do not see the treasure because we are too busy looking for it elsewhere.

The authors of the Declaration of Independence were wise. They said that our "unalienable right" was the "pursuit of happiness." They did not say, "pursuit of fun" or "pursuit of pleasure" or even "pursuit of success." They knew that none of these, nor all of these together, were synonymous with happiness. Unfortunately, Western civilization has made the mistake of equating these other pursuits with the pursuit of happiness. But the truth is, as long as we try to achieve happiness by these routes, we will never achieve it. We may certainly enjoy any of these pursuits, but we should not confuse them with happiness.

We're left with a series of questions, then: what is the source of happiness? Where do we find it? What are we missing? Who or what is to blame for our lack of happiness?

Ease of Blame

I once said, only half in jest, that there are *four* rather than three essentials of life: (1) food and water; (2) clothing; (3) shelter; and (4) *someone or something to blame.* It is surprising how easily we assign causes to things, without closer examination as to their validity. The following story exemplifies this predisposition to transfer blame to circumstances outside ourselves.

When Edgar was sixteen years old, he found himself discontent. He was doing well in school, participated in sports, and did the things most young men his age do. Edgar's parents were kind and caring. His father was a mill worker who provided adequately for his family. At the end of the workday, he would kick off his shoes and sit in front of the TV with a can of beer. His mother was a competent housewife who tended to Edgar's and his sister's needs. The family attended church services, albeit not regularly. In general, it was a pleasant home.

But Edgar was discontent. He had little interest in high school. Although his grades were above average, he was bored. He believed that once he entered college in the field of his choice, he would be more motivated. He thought he might become a pharmacist, and for the first two months in pharmacy school, he was rather enthusiastic. However, as the semester wore on, his interest waned, and he concluded that pharmacy was not his thing. He then switched to business administration, but again, as the novelty of the course wore off, he found himself brooding.

Edgar finally concluded that he was not cut out for college, and he took a job as an appliance salesman. He was quite successful, began earning good money, and felt upbeat. When he began to feel unhappy yet again, he reasoned that he was lonely. Most of his co-workers had families, and he thought that he would be happier if he were married.

So Edgar married a wonderful young woman, and he did, indeed, feel much happier. He was promoted to store manager and became a father. His life was quite busy, but when he had spaces of time, the old dejection came back. Edgar now attributed his unhappiness to the increased stress at work and to the fact that their baby had a congenital heart problem. Although the doctors reassured him that the child would have a normal life, Edgar could not help worrying. Their second child was born healthy, but his wife developed a postpartum depression that was very stressful for Edgar.

Eventually, Edgar was promoted to district manager. His income increased appreciably, and his wife's health returned to normal. When he once again felt discontent, he attributed it to the stress he was having at work: being responsible for six stores and dealing with disgruntled employees. He was also concerned about the problems their children were having at school, and that his son had been caught with marijuana.

By the time Edgar was fifty-six, most things had settled down. Both children had married and were financially independent. He had expanded the business and things were going well. Why was he still feeling unhappy?

"Of course! It's the house we are living in. Things would be so much better if we lived in the suburbs, with a state-of-the-art home and a spacious lawn." They found a plot of land, and the next three years were occupied with architects, designers, contractors, and subcontractors. There were always things going wrong, more than enough to justify discontent.

Finally, their home was complete. The carpets and furnishings were in; the drapes, lamps, and pictures were in place; and the lawn and bushes were beautiful. The first several months in the new home were great. Friends visited and commented on the beauty of their new home.

But Edgar's unhappiness returned. Now what? There was really nothing he was lacking. He began to think of the spats he had with his wife over the years, and how she never did value his business acumen. She had never really appreciated him enough. He realized something he had never considered seriously before: his marriage was a failure. The ensuing divorce, however, did not eliminate his discontent. To the contrary, he had lost the companionship of a wife who had really loved him.

Edgar then consulted a psychiatrist, who prescribed antidepressant medications, none of which relieved Edgar's discontent. Edgar also saw a psychologist, who tried to discover the roots of Edgar's unhappiness, but to no avail.

What Edgar had not considered was that there was part of him whose needs were never met. Throughout his adult life, there had always been things to which he could attribute his discontent, but it had never occurred to Edgar to think in terms of spirituality as the path to happiness.

2
Spiritual Deficiency
Syndrome

I n my early days as a psychiatrist, I joined the staff of a state mental hospital, where I was assigned to a unit of chronic patients, many of whom had been hospitalized for years. To acquaint myself with the people who would be under my care, I arranged to review their medical records and then meet with them.

When the nurse ushered one patient into my office, I exclaimed, "My God! She has no thyroid!" Her facial features were classic for someone who had severe thyroid hormone deficiency.

I reviewed this patient's medical record. She was fifty-seven and had been in the state hospital for three years. Previously, she had been treated for depression in two community hospitals, but when she had not responded to medication or electroshock treatment, she had been deemed to have an intractable depression and had been hospitalized for indefinite care. When I checked the records from the community hospitals where she had been treated, I found that *no thyroid evaluation had been done.* Severe thyroid deficiency can result in depression that will not improve with antidepressant treatment and can be cured only by supplying the missing thyroid hormone. We started her on thyroid hormone treatment immediately. Her long-term depression improved dramatically, but she had made an adjustment to the state hospital and did not feel there was a place for her in the "outside" community. The label "mentally ill" had been indelibly attached.

This case makes my point: if a person suffers from a deficiency condition, nothing other than the missing substance can remedy the condition. This patient with a thyroid deficiency had no chance of recovery without thyroid hormones. A person with an iron-deficiency anemia will not improve with all the vitamins in the world unless iron is prescribed. This is true of all vitamin and mineral deficiency conditions—and of human deficiency conditions, as well.

The problem lies in the lack of a proper diagnosis. When the cause of a condition goes unrecognized, the treatment is not going to be successful in alleviating the problem. If we are unhappy and don't recognize the cause of our condition, we will remain chronically discontent. We'll keep placing the blame on incidents and relationships, or try to find remedies in all the wrong places, and we'll still be unaware of the true cause—and we will still be unhappy.

In her marvelously wise book *My Grandfather's Blessings*, Dr. Rachel Naomi Remen puts it this way (though I emphasize certain words with italics):

> Perhaps the root cause of stress is not overbearing bosses, ill-behaved children or the breakdown of relationships. It is the loss of a sense of our soul. If so, all the ways in which we have attempted to ease stress cannot heal it at the deepest level. Stress may heal only *through the recognition that we cannot betray our spiritual nature without paying a great price*. It is not that we *have* a soul but that we *are* a soul.

What Dr. Remen calls "soul," I call the human "spirit." And it is the neglect of the human spirit that is the cause not only of stress but also of pervasive and chronic discontent. Just as a lack of essential bodily nutrients results in a deficiency condition, failure to provide the spirit with its essential nutrients results in what I call Spiritual Deficiency Syndrome (SDS). The primary symptom of SDS is *chronic discontent.*

Unfortunately, SDS is often not recognized, and many people are unaware of the true cause for their discontent. It is only natural for people to seek relief from discomfort, but the typical "reliefs" of alcohol, mood-altering drugs, sex, shopping, and eating are merely escapist techniques. Being unaware of the real reason for their unhappiness, people are likely to attribute it to what *they think* may be the cause.

However, since deficiency conditions respond *only* to administration of the specific nutrient that is lacking, the discontent of SDS can be relieved *only* by providing the spirit with its essential nutrients. That leads us to the core question: *What is essential to the human spirit?* Within the answer lies the key to happiness. But before I go any further, it is important to clarify what I mean by the "human spirit."

"Something Else"

The human spirit is an integral part of a human being, much the same as the heart, liver, eyes, and ears. The human body makes its needs known very dramatically through the feelings of hunger, thirst, anger, sex drive, pain, and weariness. We are immediately familiar with the body, and we do not have to think whether or not the body exists in reality.

The human spirit, however, although very real, is intangible. We cannot see or touch it, and it does not make its needs known as emphatically as the body does. Yet it is obvious that a human being comprises a body *plus* "something else." The physical human body is essentially an animal body, with rather minor anatomical differences. But we do have a number of abilities that distinguish us from animals. These unique features comprise the human spirit. Animals, for instance, are motivated only by self-gratification, whereas humans have the ability to give of themselves, even sacrificing their own comfort or belongings to help total strangers. These human features, these traits that make us distinct from animals and unique as human beings, are the "something else" that defines the human spirit.

In addition to greater intelligence, some of the more obvious uniquely human features include:

- the ability to be self-aware
- the ability to be humble
- the ability to choose
- the ability to be patient
- the ability to make the most out of circumstances
- the ability to improve
- the ability to be compassionate
- the ability to have perspective
- the ability to have purpose
- the ability to search for truth
- the ability to change

I group all of these features together and propose that *the sum total of all the traits that are unique to humans is what we refer to as the human spirit.* Note that I am not saying we all have all of these traits. Rather, I am saying that we all have these *abilities.* For example, a person may or may not reflect on the purpose of existence, but every human being has the *ability* to do so.

This brings us full circle back to the question of happiness.

To become complete human beings, to find happiness, we need to develop our human spirits to the fullest. This is what it means to be spiritual: to be the best we can be—to exercise all the qualities and traits that are unique to humankind and that give us the identity as human beings. This spirituality is an integral component of being human, and we cannot have true and enduring happiness without it. Just as we need to have a sufficient amount of iron for optimum function, we need to have *a sufficient amount of spirituality* to avoid the chronic discontent of Spiritual Deficiency Syndrome. To put it another way, without spirituality, the pursuit of happiness is doomed to futility.

Often, it seems the meaning of the terms *religion* and *spirituality* are confused as being the same. I do not believe that they are the same. I believe that every person can be spiritual, regardless of the degree or even presence of formal religion. And I believe that we can learn a great deal about spirituality from each other.

Now *That's* Spiritual!

One of my patients taught me a great lesson in what it means to be a spiritual person. On the day she was scheduled for a consultation, I happened to be in a bad mood. I had just bought a new automobile, fully loaded, but the cruise control was not accurate, fluctuating five miles per hour from where I set it. I was going to have to take it back to the dealer for an adjustment, which would cost me half a day.

Nora arrived for her appointment ecstatic and bubbling with happiness. She was eight months sober and was beginning to reap some of the rewards of sobriety. Her son was going to school all day, so she had found a full-time job, albeit at minimum wage. She had also found a suitable, inexpensive apartment for herself and her child. She thought she might even be able to save enough money to get her car fixed.

"What's wrong with your car?" I asked.

"There's no reverse," she said. "The reverse gear is broken."

"How can you drive without a reverse gear?" I asked.

"Oh, you have to plan things out," she said, "like how to park so you can get out without backing up. But I must remember that some people don't even have a car."

If I could have dug a hole in the ground, I would have jumped in. I was in an irritable mood because the cruise control on my new, fully loaded car was five miles per hour off, while Nora was happy with a car that did not have a reverse gear.

Nora taught me an important lesson in spirituality that day: *happiness is not having the most, but needing the least.*

Nora demonstrated spiritual happiness in yet another way. She had been treated with chemotherapy for cancer and had lost all her hair. She now regularly visits her oncologist's office to share her experience and lift up the spirits of cancer patients. She shows them a picture of her bald head when she was on chemo and says, "Look! My hair is thicker than ever! Chemotherapy was the greatest thing to happen to my hair!"

Just recently I received a Thanksgiving Day greeting from Nora: "I'm ten years sober and seven years cancer-free. Life is good. (And my car has a reverse gear!)"

Nora is a spiritual person.

There is a very moving story about a young, mentally challenged boy who was being mainstreamed in public school. One day, young Alvin was walking with his father, and they passed a field where some children were playing baseball. Alvin recognized some of them and said, "Do you think they would let me play with them?"

Alvin's father's heart sank. He knew that Alvin could not hit or catch a ball. Of course, the kids would refuse to let him play.

"Ask them, Daddy," Alvin said, "ask them."

Anticipating a negative answer, Alvin's father nevertheless asked one of the boys, "Could you let Alvin try to bat once?"

The boys looked at each other, and one of them said, "Sure! We're tied four to four and we need a good hitter."

They gave Alvin the bat and showed him how to hold it and swing. The pitcher stood six feet from the plate and softly lobbed in the ball. Alvin waved the bat at it, missing it by a mile.

"Good try," a boy said. One of the boys held Alvin's hands on the bat, and when the next pitch came, Alvin tapped it in front of the plate.

"You got a hit, Alvin! Run to first!" The pitcher retrieved the ball and threw it high over the first-baseman's head into right field.

"Run to second, Alvin!" the kids screamed. The right fielder realized what was going on, and he threw the ball far past the third-baseman.

"Run to third, Alvin!" Then, "Run home, Alvin, run home!" The catcher caught the ball and waved at Alvin when he crossed the plate, avoiding the tag.

All the kids started yelling, "Alvin got a homer! We won!" They then picked Alvin up and carried him on their shoulders in a victory march.

These kids were spiritual. They did not win the ball game, they won much more.

Yossi was born with a heart defect. Doctors told his parents that he would need a heart operation when he turned seven, and that they should have the procedure done in the United States.

Yossi's parents, both Israelis, knew no one in America, but a mutual friend put them in touch with me. The heart surgeon at Pittsburgh's Children's Hospital said that he would do the procedure.

Neither Yossi nor his parents knew a word of English, so I put the word out in Pittsburgh for Hebrew-speaking people. Twenty-nine people volunteered and gathered for an emergency meeting.

A schedule was arranged whereby the family would never be left without an interpreter. No volunteer would leave until his or her replacement came. Not only was there effective communication, but the family also received loving support during the trying two weeks of hospitalization.

Because the family had no insurance, the hospital reduced the charges to the bare minimum. The surgeon did not charge a fee. The community raised the money for the hospital bill.

These were all spiritual people.

(Years later, I visited Yossi in Israel. He was playing a vigorous game of basketball.)

At the age of forty-six, Dotty came to the Gateway Rehabilitation System in Pennsylvania for treatment. How she had survived until that age was a mystery because she had begun abusing substances at the age of fourteen, and in the years that followed, she had had countless brushes with death from accidental overdoses. Once she achieved sobriety, however, she threw herself wholeheartedly into trying to help others recover, and many people owe their lives to Dotty.

Still, she never entirely shook off the wounds and fears from her drugging days. Once, we attended a funeral of a mutual friend, and we were two out of the ten mourners in attendance. When we left the cemetery, Dotty said to me, "When I die, I want there to be a procession two miles long because I want to have made the friends I could not make when I was drugging."

At age sixty-two, Dotty was diagnosed with cancer. Her hospital room was always busy with the noise of friends visiting and trying their best to be there for her. Many of these were friends she had helped recover. Some, she had pulled back from the brink of death. To say they were all connected is a compliment to Dotty on a life lived with great purpose.

When Dotty died, she indeed had a long funeral procession, and if it was not a full two miles long, it was not much less.

During her early life, Dotty had been very much alone, disconnected, and into self-gratification. Her mind had been in a state of suspended animation from the high of drugs, and she could not relate to other people. Once she recovered, however, Dotty loved and was loved. She was not alone in life or abandoned in death. By helping others, by looking outside herself, she was able to connect with people.

Dotty was a spiritual person.

A rabbi was once sitting with several of his students. He said to one student, "Could you please bring me a cup of coffee with two spoons of sugar?" The student brought the coffee, and the rabbi sipped it slowly, continuing his discourse with the students.

A bit later, the rabbi went into the kitchen himself for coffee, and just as he was about to put the sugar in the coffee, his wife said, "Don't do that! That's salt, not sugar." It turned out that the student had mistaken the salt for sugar and had put two spoons of salt into the rabbi's coffee.

"How could you drink the coffee with all that salt in it?" the rabbi's wife asked.

"What else could I have done?" the rabbi asked. "If I had refused to drink it, that would have embarrassed the student who made the mistake."

This rabbi was a spiritual person. I am privileged to have known him.

Now for a bit of nostalgia.

When I was seven, Reuben, an elderly worshiper in my father's synagogue, invited me to his home for potato pancakes. This became a weekly event. Every Tuesday evening was potato pancake night. I would watch Reuben grate the potatoes (there were no food processors then) and fry them to a crisp brown.

I often looked at a picture of Reuben, his wife, and their seven children. Except for two sons, all had died prematurely. Reuben was blind in his left eye and wore a thick lens over his right eye. "I became blind from crying," Reuben would explain.

If any human being had a right to be not only discontented with life, but also bitter and angry, it was Reuben. But as a sensitive seven-year-old, I did not detect any bitterness. Before services on Saturday morning, I would sit with Reuben as he read the entire book of Psalms. He shared with the psalmist both his expression of anguish and his hope for joy. If Reuben had been bitter, the potato pancakes could not have been as delicious.

Reuben was a spiritual person.

Another personal story.

After serving as a rabbi for several years, I decided to go to medical school. I had two children, and supporting the family while going to medical school was going to be a challenge. My congregation was not particularly wealthy, but the membership helped me with the tuition. Nevertheless, in my third year I was in arrears of two trimester's tuition, and I asked the administration to be patient with me.

One Sunday, I called home at lunchtime, and my wife said, "What would you do if you had four thousand dollars?"

I said, "We'd take a trip around the world, but I don't have the time for fantasy now."

"Well, you've got four thousand dollars from Danny Thomas," she said.

"Who is Danny Thomas?" I asked.

"You know, the television comedian," she said. I did not know. The medical school curriculum did not provide time for watching TV.

"Listen to this item in today's paper: 'At a meeting with officials of Marquette University, Danny Thomas was told about a young rabbi who is struggling to get through medical school. "How much does your rabbi need to finish?" Danny Thomas asked. "About four thousand dollars," the officials said. "Tell your rabbi he's got it," Danny Thomas said.'"

Several days later I received a letter from Danny Thomas, with a profound apology for the item appearing in the paper. "There was a reporter at our meeting, but it didn't occur to me that he would publish this. I'm sorry if it caused you embarrassment."

A year later, I met Danny Thomas in the TV studio. I told him that there was no reason for an apology. "The papers always print the sensationalism of bad things that happen. Why shouldn't they print the good things, too?"

Danny shook his head. "We in the entertainment industry make our living by publicity, and there are many things we do for publicity. This was something I wanted to do because it felt right, and I did not want it to be a publicity stunt."

Danny Thomas dedicated himself to the development of the St. Jude Children's Research Hospital in Memphis for research and treatment of children's malignancies.

Danny Thomas was a spiritual person.

And then there was Donna.

After several years of marriage, Donna became concerned when she had not conceived. She made the rounds to all the specialists. Her family physician, after receiving all the reports, said to her, "Donna, you need to accept this. You will never be able to carry a child."

Donna was crushed. However, she and her husband adopted a baby boy and subsequently a baby girl.

When Donna turned forty, she decided it was time that she give up smoking. She went through several weeks of much discomfort, but eventually felt better. Several months later, she again began having unpleasant feelings, and when she consulted her physician, she found out she was pregnant!

Donna was overjoyed by this miracle. She knew she would have a son, who was going to be a Rhodes scholar like his daddy. "But my world turned dark when they put the baby in my arms the first time. He was a Down syndrome child. I was bitter and angry. 'God, why did you do this to me? I had already resigned myself to not having a child. Why did you raise my hopes, only to deliver this crushing blow to me?'

"Every night, Ed and I prayed over the crib. 'Dear God, you can do anything. Change him.' Then one day God answered our prayers—by changing *us*!

"Now, if that child did not come into the world for any other reason but what I will tell you now, it was all worth it. Because when I sit in the rocker, holding Andy, and I see the way his eyes are funny shaped and some other ways in which he is different, and I know how much I love that child with all his shortcomings, that's when I can understand that God can love me, even with all my shortcomings."

Donna is a spiritual person.

Now for the other side.

Brian consulted me because he was contemplating suicide. "My father is crazy," Brian said. "He is eighty-four and has built up a billion-dollar empire. If he lived for a thousand years, he could not consume a fraction of his wealth. Yet, he goes to the office every day to make more money. What for?

"My share of the business is already far beyond what I will ever need. I have two condos, one on the West coast and the other on the Riviera. I have a stable full of horses. I don't want to make more money. What's the point?

"When I get into a plane, it's not to go anywhere, but to get away from where I am. I see no point in continuing with life."

Brian was discontented to the point of contemplating suicide.

"But, with all your extra money," I said, "just think of how much good you can do! Think of how many hungry people you could feed, and how much valuable medical research you could sponsor. You would even have good reason to generate more money for worthy causes."

Brian looked at me with a bewildered expression. "Give away my money? Why would I want to do that?"

Brian was *not* a spiritual person, and he was bitterly discontented.

Faithfulness to Life

Spirituality and happiness are inseparable. If someone is missing an arm or a leg or has no vision, this does not detract from his "person-hood." He can very well be a whole person in spite of a physical lack. However, if someone lacks spirituality, this detracts from her very essence as a human being. She is not complete—and she is definitely not happy!

Consider for a moment another of Dr. Remen's insights from *My Grandfather's Blessings* (though I emphasize certain words with italics):

> We are a culture that values mastery and control, that cultivates self-sufficiency, competence, independence. *But in the shadow of these values lies a profound rejection of our human wholeness....* In a highly technological world, we may forget our own goodness and place value instead on our skills and our expertise. But it is not our expertise that will restore the world. The future may depend less on our expertise than on our *faithfulness to life.*

"Faithfulness to life." Faithfulness to being the persons we were created to be. Faithfulness to living our potential. This is the essence of a spiritual person: someone who is in the process of becoming *the best person he or she can be.* Many people have *some* spirituality, but not enough to satisfy the spirit. To be truly happy, we need to be continually in the process of exercising and implementing the elements of the human spirit to the best of our abilities. True happiness—and true spirituality—comes from becoming the best human beings we can be.

Part 2

The UNIQUE HUMAN SPIRIT

3

The Ability to
Be Self-Aware

If the source of true happiness lies in becoming the *best human beings we can be*—in other words, self-improvement, which leads to self-fulfillment—then it makes sense to take a closer look at the unique traits that make us human. Each ability we humans have is an area where we can strive to be better. And each area where we don't strive for self-fulfillment is an area ripe for discontent.

But before I say another word about "being better," I want to be very clear that I'm not talking about "being perfect." In fact, if anything, I'm talking about just the opposite—the spirituality of *imperfection*. Ernest Kurtz has written a wonderful book with that title in which he extensively comments on the potential that can be found within our imperfection.

> To deny our errors is to deny ourselves, for to be human is to be imperfect. To be human ... is to be broken and ache for wholeness, to hurt and to try to find a way to healing through the hurt.... A spirituality of imperfection suggests that spirituality's first step involves facing oneself squarely, seeing one's self as one is: mixed-up, paradoxical, incomplete, and imperfect. Flawedness is the first fact about human beings. And paradoxically, in that imperfect foundation we

27

find not despair but joy. For it is only within the reality of our imperfection that we can find the peace and serenity we crave.

Then he cites the following story.

Rabbi Elimelech of Lizensk said, "I am sure of my share in Heaven. When I stand before the Heavenly Tribunal, I will be asked, 'Did you learn, as is duty bound?' To this I will answer, 'No.' Again, I will be asked, 'Did you pray, as is duty bound?' Again my answer will be, 'No.' The third question will be, 'Did you do good deeds, as is duty bound?' For the third time, I will answer, 'No.' The judgment will be, 'He may enter Heaven, for he speaks the truth.'"

In order for any of us to be the *best person we can be*, it is essential that we have an accurate awareness of ourselves—of both our shortcomings and our skills. If someone who is tone-deaf thinks that she can become a soprano virtuoso, she will be very frustrated because that is not "what she can be." On the other hand, a person who is highly talented musically but fails to develop that talent may be equally discontent because he has not maximized his potential.

It stands to reason that we cannot fulfill our capabilities if we are unaware of them. Such lack of awareness is fairly common. What is surprising is this paradox: *people who are most gifted may have profound feelings of inferiority.*

Janice was a board-certified pediatrician who suffered from severe depression. She was clearly a very accomplished woman, yet, when asked to list her character strengths, she could not think of anything to say. I pointed out to her that graduating summa cum laude and receiving the Phi Beta Kappa award were evidence of a high intellect, and that this was an undeniable character asset. Janice responded with a deep sigh: "When they told me about the Phi Beta Kappa award," she said, "I knew they had made a mistake." Her husband, Alex, constantly berated her, and she believed his disparagement. Her excellence as a physician had little impact on her self-esteem.

Other people may be aware of some of their character assets but unaware of others. Dr. J. is a classic example.

Dr. J. would begin his rounds in the hospital at seven a.m. After seeing his patients, he taught medical students and student nurses, and he also sat on various hospital committees. He would leave for his private office at one p.m. and return to the hospital at six p.m., often remaining until midnight. The nurses assumed that Dr. J.'s wife was a terrible person: why else would he avoid going home?

Dr. J. asked me to see his wife because she was depressed. I found out that she was a very gentle woman, nothing like the nurses imagined. She told me how much she wanted a shoulder to lean on once in a while, but that her husband was never there for her. Basically, she said, their two children grew up without a father. If they were sick, Dr. J. would take care of them, but he never showed any interest in their schoolwork or social lives. He was never there to guide them.

Dr. J.'s low self-esteem was compartmentalized. He knew that he was competent as a physician, but he did not feel he had anything to offer as a *person*. He was comfortable in the hospital, where he felt capable of doing what was expected of him. However, he did not feel he had anything to offer as a husband and father, and because he felt inadequate at home, he avoided his family. Dr. J. fulfilled himself only as a physician, but not as a person, husband, and father.

Self-esteem is one of those terms that we seem to be always redefining, but I think it is fair to say that *we can't have self-esteem until we can be aware of our potential*. Self-awareness is a uniquely human ability, and we will never find happiness until we get to know who we really are.

The "Real" You

Self-awareness may not be easy to come by. It requires conscientious reflection, which many people may be reluctant to do. I discovered this the hard way.

I had spent three years of grueling work as director of a three-hundred-bed psychiatric hospital. Not only were my days hectic, with constant demands by patients, doctors, nurses, families, social workers, lawyers, and probation officers, but my nights were even worse. Our hospital was the receiving center and the only emergency service for a population of four million. On a good night, I would be awoken six times. On a bad night, it could be fifteen times.

Not surprisingly, I decided to use my two-week vacation for absolute rest. I had no desire to do any sightseeing, boating, hiking, or anything else. I only wished to be left alone, to recline in an easy chair, to do nothing more than breathe. I needed two weeks of total inactivity.

All the possible vacation spots my friends suggested seemed far too active for me. I finally settled on Hot Springs, Arkansas, a rather small town whose economy of horse racing does not begin until mid-February. In December, there is nothing to do other than drink the naturally heated spring water and soak in a tub of mineral water. The latter was particularly inviting because I hoped that the healing waters would relieve my chronic low-back pain.

I was led into a tiny cubicle where there was a whirlpool bath. Immersed in the soothing warm water, I felt I was in paradise. I was beyond the reach of patients, nurses, and all the others who encroached on my time and energies. This surely must be what Nirvana is like.

After about six minutes, I alighted from the tub. The attendant asked me, "Where are you going, sir?"

"To whatever is next," I said.

The attendant replied, "You cannot go on with the treatment until you've been in the whirlpool bath for twenty-five minutes."

I returned to the tub, but after five more minutes, I said to the attendant, "I have to get out of here." It was only because I hoped the treatment would relieve my backache that I stayed in the tub for another fifteen minutes—which seemed like an eternity.

Later that day I reflected on what was a rude awakening. I had tolerated the stress, frenzy, and hectic pace at work for *three years*, but could not tolerate paradise for more than six minutes! What was wrong?

If you ask people how they relax, one person might say, "I like to read a good book." Another might say, "I play golf." Yet another does needlework, or listens to music, or watches television. These are all pleasant activities, but in each case, the person is *doing something* in order to relax. Their attention is focused on something: the book, the golf ball, the needlework. These are *diversions* rather than true relaxation. True relaxation is the absence of doing anything.

In my little cubicle, I had been deprived of anything to which I could direct my attention. There was no one to talk to, nothing to read, nothing to listen to, nothing to look at. Without anything to divert my attention, I was left with only *myself*. And the hard truth was that I was in a small space with someone I did not like very much. No wonder I wanted to get away.

This led me to investigate what there was about me that I so despised that I could not tolerate my own presence, and I embarked on a self-awareness program. I found out that the self-image I had carried for thirty-eight years was erroneous. When I eventually discovered the "real" me, I liked myself much more. The proof: I have been back to Hot Springs several times, and each time I've thoroughly enjoyed a full twenty-five minutes in the whirlpool bath.

A Trick Mirror

Low self-esteem is very common and may occur without a discernible cause. We can understand why a child who has been subject to neglect and abuse might develop feelings of inferiority. But in my case, I grew up in a wonderful home, with loving, caring parents. In fact, I was my father's favorite. Yet not only had I developed feelings of inferiority, *but I was unaware that I felt this way about myself.* Subsequently, in my psychiatric practice, I have found that many people harbor a hidden, erroneous, negative self-image.

I once came across a story about a child who was raised in a home that had only one mirror: it was a carnival trick mirror that distorted the image. Every time the child looked in the mirror, he saw himself as a grotesque, ugly creature. Eventually, he avoided the mirror.

When he grew up, he avoided contact with people because he knew his abhorrent appearance would elicit reactions of disgust, which would hurt him deeply. He lived in an isolated hut, venturing out to get provisions only late at night when few people were around.

One time the grocer asked him, "Why do you only come so late at night? I never see you during the day."

The man answered, "I can't stand the reactions of people who will look at me."

"Reactions?" the grocer asked. "What kind of reactions?"

"People would be frightened, even revolted, by my appearance."

"Why do you say that?" the grocer asked.

"Are you trying to be kind to me?" the man said. "I know what I look like, and I know how people would react to a grotesque-looking person like me."

The grocer replied, "I don't know what you're talking about. There is nothing grotesque about you. You're a rather handsome person."

"Thank you for trying to make me feel better," the man said and turned to leave.

The grocer came from behind the counter, took hold of the man, and protested, "This is simply crazy. I don't know where you got this nutty idea that you're grotesque. Here, just look in this mirror."

"No, that's one thing I will not do. I've suffered enough from looking in the mirror."

The grocer pulled the man over to a mirror and challenged, "Look! What do you see?"

The man said, "I don't know where you got a mirror that could change my grotesque features that way. Anyway, thanks for trying."

The story makes the point well: it was difficult for this man to achieve a valid self-awareness because he believed he would find only ugliness. He had Spiritual Deficiency Syndrome. People who have a negative self-image, whether they are aware of it or not, will behave as though the negatives are their reality, which may result in self-defeating behavior—and much unhappiness.

It is important to correct a distorted self-concept because the behavior due to low self-esteem may be a self-reinforcing vicious cycle. For example, people who suffer low self-esteem and who anticipate being rejected by others will often act in such a way as to precipitate the very rejection they fear.

A classic example of this is T.J., who was a twenty-one-year-old college sophomore. T.J. was bright, handsome, and witty, and he had a 4.0 average. However, T.J.'s self-concept was the polar opposite of the truth: he thought of himself as dull and unattractive.

Then T.J. met Carol, a student nurse, and he managed to build up the courage to ask her for a date. He was thrilled when she accepted, and they had a wonderful time. She accepted additional requests for dates, but as he grew fond of her, he began to be haunted by the feeling that she would eventually reject him. Why would Carol be interested in an ongoing relationship with him when she could do so much better?

Every time he called her, he anticipated being rejected. Surely, this would be the time when she would say, "T.J., I've been trying to avoid hurting your feelings, but I can't see you anymore." Given the way T.J. felt about himself, the impending rejection was a certainty.

Finally, the tension of the anticipated rejection became so unbearable that T.J. sent a telegram to Carol's father: "Congratulations. In seven months you will be a grandfather." Carol called and told him never to call her again.

Understandably, T.J. was deeply affected by the rejection that *he had brought about*. His low self-esteem was now depressed an additional notch. It is characteristic of low self-esteem that it feeds on itself and has a downward progression into more self-defeating behaviors of Spiritual Deficiency Syndrome.

"I'm No Good"

There is one self-defeating behavior that is of overwhelming importance and can have far-reaching negative effects—the *reaction of shame*. The terms *shame* and *guilt* are often used interchangeably. People might say, "I am ashamed of what I did," but what they really mean is, "I feel guilty about what I did." Although the two terms are confused colloquially, there is a significant difference. Guilt is a feeling we have when we have done something wrong. Guilt can be constructive when it leads us to make amends and to correct a mistake by apologizing or making restitution. Guilt can also be a deterrent. We tend to avoid a particular act if we know it will cause the painful feeling of guilt. Because guilt is for an *act*, it is remediable. Making proper amends and resolving not to repeat the act can relieve our guilt.

Shame, however, is altogether different. Shame refers to feeling that *"I'm no good."* Whereas guilt is the result of an act, the feeling of shame may occur in absence of any wrongdoing. A child who is humiliated by parents, teachers, or others may develop the feeling "I am bad." To put it another way, guilt is the feeling "I *made* a mistake. I *did* something bad." Shame is the feeling "I *am* a mistake. I *am* bad." While we can take steps to remove guilt, the feeling that "there is something inherently bad about me" is much more difficult to overcome. Shame not only leaves no room for correction, but it also imposes a heavy burden that interferes with living in a self-fulfilling manner—and certainly puts a damper on happiness.

Since our identity is a major part of our reality, perceiving ourselves as inherently bad is a distortion of reality. We will never find the elusive quality of "happiness" until we have a valid perception of reality, which requires a valid perception of ourselves. Yet years of negative thinking are not easily undone. In the twelve-step recovery program, one of the steps is to do a "fearless moral inventory." People who have a negative concept of themselves may be very reluctant to engage in self-awareness, fearing that they will be depressed by what they will discover. But, in order to be self-aware, we need to overcome our fear of self-discovery.

The Value of a Sandwich

In a *Calvin and Hobbes* cartoon strip, Calvin asks Hobbes what he wishes for.

"A sandwich," Hobbes replies.

"Is that all you can think of?" Calvin asks. "Why, I would wish for a spaceship of my own, a ballpark and a football field of my own, and a gazillion dollars!"

In the final cartoon frame, Hobbes is seen eating a sandwich and quietly saying, "I got my wish."

Discovering the "real" you requires a correct assessment of reality. As much as it is not healthy to distort the negatives, it is also not healthy to distort the positives. A delusion is a delusion, and a delusion of grandiosity is every bit as unrealistic as a delusion of inferiority.

A psychiatrist once began an interview by saying to the client, "Tell me your problem."

The client responded, "I have a forty-four-room mansion, located on five hundred acres of beautiful countryside. I have a housekeeper, cook, governess, gardener, and chauffeur, and I own two luxury automobiles."

The psychiatrist interrupted him. "So, what is the problem?"

"I'm just about to get to that," the client said. "You see, I earn only $150 a week."

Just as a person, who has unwarranted feelings of inferiority and inadequacy is going to get into trouble, so too is the person who has grandiose delusions of being a billionaire. Self-awareness is knowing both our potential and our limitations.

This situation exemplifies the aphorism "The truth will set you free." A distorted self-image is a distortion of truth, and this may blind us to self-defeating behavior. Knowing the truth about ourselves releases our energies. When we are free, we can develop our potential to its fullest.

4

The Ability to Be Humble

I don't know whether animals are vain (except, perhaps, strutting peacocks), but they certainly know nothing of humility. This is an ability only human beings have, and it is one of the traits that contributes to being a better person, a spiritual person, and, therefore, a happier person.

It is rather unpleasant to be in the presence of a vain person. Think of the person at work who never tires of telling you how great he is. Or the woman whose entire demeanor is self-aggrandizing. Or your neighbor who tends to belittle those around him by being condescending, a name-dropper, or a spinner of tall tales.

It is also rather unpleasant to *be* a vain person. Vanity is often the hallmark of a narcissistic personality. The term *narcissism* derives from the Greek myth about Narcissus, who was very handsome, and when he saw his reflection in the water, he fell in love with himself. Narcissistic people are infatuated with themselves and they never see anything wrong with themselves. They expect everyone to respect—nay, adore—them and are easily offended when they think people do not appreciate them enough.

Although the grandiosity of vain or narcissistic people would seem to indicate that they think they are the greatest, the truth is just the opposite. Their grandiosity is a defense to protect themselves from their deep feelings of inferiority. They, in fact, suffer from the chronic afflictions of Spiritual Deficiency Syndrome.

It is impossible to satisfy narcissistic people. Whatever you do for them, it is not enough. Regardless of how much you tell them that you love them, it is never enough because their underlying belief that they are unlovable does not allow them to accept any reassurance. Surprisingly, the term *narcissistic* is actually inaccurate. Narcissistic people do *not* love themselves. To the contrary, they generally suffer from very low self-esteem and seek universal approval and adoration to give themselves a sense of worthiness. The self-centeredness of narcissistic people makes it impossible for them to be spiritual—and impossible for them to be happy.

Humble Enough to Learn

It is normal to wish to be recognized, and this does not constitute vanity. The problem arises when people who suffer low self-esteem feel desperate to validate themselves as worthy human beings. People who know their own worth do not need to flaunt their abilities. To the contrary, they are secure enough to always be teachable.

Several months into my psychiatric training, I received a call from a relative in New York whose husband had developed a severe depression. At the time, I was studying a text on the physiologic treatments of depression, written by Dr. Lothar Kalinowsky, an international authority on the subject, and I suggested that my relative consult him. Several days later, I was surprised to receive a call from this internationally renowned psychiatrist. He said that the available medications at that time were slow-working and, because of the depth of my relative's depression, he felt that several electroshock treatments would hasten recovery. What was my opinion?

I said, "Dr. Kalinowsky, you may be under the impression that I am a practicing psychiatrist. I am just at the beginning of my training, and as yet I know very little about electroshock."

Dr. Kalinowsky said, "Yes, I know electroshock well, but you know this patient better than I do."

I then said, "I have only one concern. He is a brilliant man, but he has always sought ways to avoid responsibility. I am concerned that if he has electroshock, he may say that his brain was affected, hence he can no longer be expected to function in a responsible position."

Dr. Kalinowsky said, "Yes, yes. You are right. No electroshock. We will try to treat him with medication."

I immediately went to the chairman of the Department of Psychiatry and said, "Guess who called me for a consultation!"

He smiled when I told him and said, "The only psychiatrist who would ask the opinion of a first-year resident is the one who wrote the book. He does not feel that asking someone of lesser stature for an opinion will reflect negatively on his capabilities."

People who feel secure can be humble. They have no need to validate themselves at the expense of others. Humble people are always learning, whereas vain people may believe they know all there is to know about a subject, and their minds may be closed to fresh ideas.

Since one of the keys to self-fulfillment is to seek to be the best we can be, vain people run into a roadblock right from the start: if they think they have already achieved the superlative, they will not see any need to be "better"!

Humble Enough to Ask for Help

The other problem of vanity is that it leads people to think they must be totally self-sufficient, that accepting help from anyone is beneath their dignity. Vain people may refuse legitimate help when they need it.

Bonnie was in her first year of recovery from alcoholism when she confided in a friend that she had slept three winter nights in an unheated apartment. There had been an extended frigid spell, and her furnace had broken down. Because there was a backlog of calls for service, the repairman had been unable to get to her home for four days.

Her friend exclaimed, "You could have called me or any of our friends and stayed with us!"

But Bonnie's response was, "No, I don't like to impose on anyone."

When I heard this, I called Bonnie and told her that I was disappointed because I had hoped to be able to call on her to help newcomers in recovery.

Bonnie was nonplussed. "But, Doctor, you can call me anytime. I'll be glad to help!"

"No, I can't," I replied. "If you cannot accept help, you cannot give it."

A humble person can ask for and accept legitimate help, and can, therefore, give it in a manner that others will accept it. A vain person may help others only because it engenders a feeling of superiority. This kind of help is tainted and may not accomplish its purpose because the beneficiary may detect a feeling of condescension. The ability to be humble is an important fundamental to the pursuit of happiness. Being able to ask for help is not only one of the ways we can connect with other people, but it is also how we learn and grow to be better human beings.

Humble Enough to Admit Mistakes

In Ernest Kurtz's book *The Spirituality of Imperfection*, he relates this marvelous quote from the commissioner of baseball, Francis T. Vincent, Jr.:

> Baseball teaches us, or has taught most of us, how to deal with failure. We learn at a very young age that failure is the norm in baseball, and precisely because we have failed, we hold in high regard those who fail less often—those who hit safely in only one out of

three chances and become star players. I also find it fascinating that baseball, alone in sport, considers errors to be part of the game, part of its rigorous growth.

If we were looking for a statement that sums up the human condition, it might be exactly this: errors are part of the game! Any discussion about "being the best we can be" has to include this codicil: the "best we can be" is *not* perfect. We will make errors. We will make mistakes. But the corollary is that admitting our mistakes is also uniquely human and is, therefore, a feature of spirituality and human fulfillment.

It is only natural to wish to be right. However, humble people are not threatened by the awareness of and admission of a mistake or even a wrong deed. Not only do they recognize human fallibility, but they also recognize the benefits of confession and penitence.

The humble position of admitting a mistake has many practical advantages. For starters, people tend to forgive someone who owns up to a mistake. It is reported that physicians who admit a mistake are less likely to be sued for malpractice. It is when physicians are adamant that they are right that the plaintiffs find experts who will testify that they are wrong.

Then there is the benefit of healing. Needless to say, repetition of mistakes may take a heavy toll. When we are aware of a mistake and ask for forgiveness, we are taking precautions against its recurrence. Admitting a mistake is particularly important in marriage. Countless marriages might have been saved if spouses had only said, "I'm sorry, I was wrong."

Acknowledging a mistake or a wrongdoing can also be extremely advantageous in character refinement. While most of us would never think of committing a heinous crime, we might be tempted to "fudge" the truth a little once in a while—on a time card, or taxes, or a business transaction, for example. If we can admit that these "minor" dishonest practices are as wrong as a heinous crime, then we are all the better persons for it.

This insight came to me at an AA meeting, when a man who was sober for twenty years said, "The man I once was, drank, and the man I once was, will drink again. If I am not drinking now, it is because my character is such that it does not allow drinking. If my character goes back to what it once was, I will drink again."

Admitting our mistakes and resolving *not* to do them again is an inadequate deterrent to repeating them. We need to take it one step further: we need to humbly refine our characters so that the objectionable act becomes an impossibility. This is true penitence, and therein lie the seeds of happiness and our dignity as human beings.

5

The Ability
to Choose

One of the components of the spirit is the uniquely human *ability to choose* by use of our intellect. In contrast, animals have no choice because they are dominated by their strong bodily drives. They cannot choose on the basis of right and wrong, good and evil. Freedom to choose our actions is distinctly human.

Some psychologists maintain that human behavior is on the same plane as that of animals, and that our freedom of choice is an illusion. They argue that humans have a number of drives, and when some of these conflict, the stronger one wins. They claim that because we are conscious of what we are doing, we may *think* we are making a free choice, but this is an illusion because our choices are really the result of internal drives.

Choice Is Greater Than Instinct

I do not subscribe to this theory. Rather, I believe that our entire concept of human responsibility is based on the assumption that we are *not* at the mercy of our impulses, that we *do* have the freedom to choose and determine much of our behavior.

That said, I need to add that some things that appear to be choices are not uniquely human acts because they are shared with animals. For example, a person may "choose" not to do something because of fear. That is not distinctly human because animals, too, may be discouraged from gratifying a drive by fear. If a hungry jackal foraging for food spies a delectable carcass that is being feasted on by a ferocious tiger, the jackal will not attempt to eat it. The jackal is not deterred by an ethical principle. It abstains from satisfying its hunger because it is afraid of getting killed by the tiger. Fear as a deterrent of behavior is an animal trait. It is the dominance of the biological fear of being killed that is greater than the biological urge to eat.

For humans, however, choice is greater than instinct. Choosing means applying our intellect to do what is moral and ethical—even if it defies strong bodily drives and urges.

Here are two examples that illustrate the difference between instinct and choice. In the first example, an employee of a financial firm that turns over millions of dollars every day may know how to transfer money from other accounts into his. He is greedy and craves wealth. However, he realizes that the auditors may be savvy about computer crime, and that if the transactions are traced to him, his ill-begotten embezzled funds would be confiscated, and he would be fined and sentenced to prison. Because he fears the punishment, he does not yield to the craving for wealth. This is *not* a uniquely human choice because animals, too, are deterred by fear of punishment.

A uniquely human choice is when a person acts ethically, in defiance of a desire, even if there is no possibility of punishment. In the second example, a married man who lives in Maine is attending a convention in Hawaii, where no one knows him. He has a desire to have a sexual affair, and there might not be negative consequences because no one back home would ever know. However, he refrains from yielding to his desire because he believes it to be morally wrong. That is an ethical choice that befits the dignity of a human being.

The importance of choice as a component of human dignity is discussed by the psychiatrist Viktor Frankl, who relates that when he was in a concentration camp, the Nazis were able to take everything away from him, but they had no control over his attitude. Even if he were put to death, he had the choice of how he would face death. No one could deprive him of this uniquely human feature, the ability to choose.

Because the ability to make moral and ethical choices is uniquely human, it is an important component of spirituality—and an essential element of human happiness.

Choices, Choices, Who's Got the Choices?

The freedom to choose is one of the most cherished human values. That is one reason why slavery is so abominable—because it deprives people of their right to make choices. Most of our waking hours are spent making choices. We choose what to wear, what to eat, and with whom to associate. Even when we get up and go to work, we have made a choice: we could have stayed in bed all day.

Yet as precious as the ability and right to choose is, it is rather surprising how readily we yield it. Take the "workaholic," who seems unable to detach herself from the office. She has to have her cell phone on at all times, to be in frequent touch with the office when she is on vacation, to call the office many times each day. She has yielded her ability to choose and become a slave to the office.

Or what about the man who is addicted to making money? We all need money for the necessities of life, for some luxuries, and to put away for a rainy day. But what if someone has more than enough money for all these, yet exerts himself to make more money? When the multibillionaire J. Paul Getty was asked, "How much money is enough?" he answered, "Just a bit more."

There is an anecdote about a psychiatrist who asked the man who was consulting him, "What is your problem?"

"I don't have any problems," the man said.

"Then why have you come to see me?" the psychiatrist asked.

"My family made me come. They think I have a problem," the man replied.

"And what does your family think is wrong with you?" the psychiatrist asked.

"They think there is something wrong with me because I like pancakes."

"That is absurd," the psychiatrist said. "There is nothing wrong with liking pancakes. Why, I like pancakes myself."

The man's eyes brightened. "You really do?" he responded. "Then you must come to my house. I have crates full of pancakes in my attic."

If a person has so many billions of dollars that, even if he and his entire family lived a thousand years, they could not consume more than a small fraction of the wealth, yet he vigorously exerts himself to make more money, how is that really different from the person collecting pancakes in the attic? People who are addicted to making money that they cannot use have surrendered their ability to make an intelligent choice.

The fallacy of addictions was well put by Matthew Kelly in his book *The Rhythm of Life*: "You can never get enough of what you don't really need."

Although we put a priority on our freedom—even go to war or risk our lives for it—we may submit to habits that are every bit as tyrannical as a dictator. Every normal human being, for instance, wants to avoid premature death and the suffering of lung cancer, emphysema, and heart disease. Yet, you will see people standing in front of an office building in subzero weather, shivering with cold, while they poison themselves with nicotine. They may say, "I wish I could stop smoking, but I just can't." They have surrendered their free will to this deadly habit. This is equally true of other addictions, such as alcohol, drugs, or compulsive gambling. They all cause symptoms of Spiritual Deficiency Syndrome.

We sometimes like to think that we do *not* have a choice. Children—and, let's face it, adults, too—often blame others for their behavior, saying the equivalent of, "He made me do it." While it may be much easier to attribute our choices to forces outside ourselves, we are responsible for our actions precisely *because* we have the ability to make choices. Exercising free will and making choices are of pivotal importance to our identity and happiness as human beings.

Science defines and classifies human beings as *Homo sapiens* (from the Latin *sapere*, "to know"), which makes intelligence the single defining feature of humans. I think that *Homo "chooser"* (or whatever the word for *choice* is in Latin) would be more appropriate. Even if an animal were to gain intelligence, it would not be human. The ability to choose freely is what makes us human.

A Better Choice

Not only is it important to protect our right to choose, but it is also important to understand *why* we choose the way we do. To do that, we need to understand something about the intricacies and marvelous ways in which the human mind operates.

We know that the body has many defenses against disease. Many diseases are a result of the failure of the defense system. We are constantly surrounded by a host of bacteria and viruses, many of which can be lethal. Indeed, we carry some of these in our bodies, yet we may be in excellent health. The reason for this is that the body's defense mechanisms keep these pathogenic germs at bay. When a germ tries to invade the body tissues, the immune system attacks it, and white blood cells from remote parts of the body go to the site and destroy the germ. All the while, we are totally unaware of the defenses that are operating to protect us from disease.

Much the same happens psychologically. Similar to the physical defenses of the immune system and the marshalling of white blood cells, we protect our conscious minds from ideas that are alien to us, or feelings that would cause us great anxiety, by diverting them from our conscious minds and depositing them into our unconscious minds. The psychological term for this is "repression," and it occurs *even when we are not aware that we are repressing something*. The problem is that repressed ideas or emotions do not just lie there, but rather, like a jack-in-the box, they accumulate until they are pushed upward and seek expression. The repressive mechanism is the psychological lid on the jack-in-the-box, and when that mechanism no longer works, the results may not be what we would choose.

On the other side of the continuum is the possibility of *suppressing* an idea or emotion. Suppression is different from repression because when we suppress something, we are *aware* that we are suppressing it. In other words, we are making a conscious choice.

Look at the difference between *suppression* and *repression* of anger. A boss provokes an employee, who becomes very angry. The employee has an urge to tell the boss what he thinks of him, but realizes that this would cost him his job. In order to keep his job, he chooses to *suppress* his anger. He is well aware of it.

The employee understands that, as a human being, he has an animal body, and that in the animal, anger is associated with the urge to attack. He may further reason, "Okay, that urge comes from the animal component of me, and I am not a horrible person for having this urge." In other words, he does not have to disown or repress it. "But," he may say to himself, "I am a human being, not an animal. I can control my behavior, I can make choices. I don't go around killing people whom I don't like." He can then can make the choice to *suppress* the thought.

Or think of a mother who provokes her daughter. The daughter believes it is wrong to feel hostile toward a parent, so her psychological defense apparatus quickly represses and pushes her anger toward her mother into the unconscious. The daughter does not shout at the mother, but begins to be resistant in a passive way. For example, the mother may ask her to go to the store for an ingredient she needs for dinner. The daughter dillydallies and does not return promptly. The mother is frustrated, waiting in the kitchen for the missing ingredient. When the daughter finally returns, she gives some excuse for the delay. She has acted out her anger toward her mother, even though she does not recognize her behavior as an expression of her anger.

A better choice—one that would have resulted in both the mother and the daughter being much happier—would have been for the daughter to say, "Gee, Mom, do I have to go? I don't want to miss the end of this program. Can't you cook it without this ingredient?"

The mother might respond, "Sorry, honey, I've got to have supper on the table by six o'clock, and I can't cook this dish without it."

The daughter might say, "Okay, I'll go, but that food isn't going to taste good to me!" This is not a disrespectful response; it is an appropriate expression of anger.

The mother could then respond, "Thanks, honey. I'm sorry to take you away from the program, but supper depends on this. Everyone will appreciate you for doing this." By responding this way, the daughter may even be able to let go of some of her anger.

It is the human *spirit* that enables us to be masters over our instincts. By suppressing rather than repressing, we exercise a degree of control and choice that contributes to our spirituality and, ultimately, to our happiness. Every time we exercise our ability to choose, we are fulfilling ourselves as spiritual human beings.

6

The Ability to
Be Patient

Animals cannot postpone. They promptly go after what they desire. We humans, on the other hand, may want to do something,
but we also have the ability to decide to delay or forgo it. The ability
to practice patience is a uniquely human trait.

Yet having patience is anything but easy! The speed of technology
has had an impact on our ability to be patient. Instant foods, microwaves, e-mail, and jet flights have resulted in a cultural obsession
with speed. We have all experienced the frustration at an airport
when it is announced that there will be a twenty-minute delay in
departure; or when we're caught in a traffic jam that puts us behind
by fifteen minutes; or when we are forced to use a dial-up service
instead of broadband and have to wait longer for something to
download.

Even in our everyday living, we're in a hurry. How many of us
make a mad dash when we see the elevator door about to close? This
was habitual with me, but then reason set in. I realized that the next
elevator was rarely more than a minute or two away. So I decided not
to exert myself and make the mad dash. However, for a few days I had
to hold on to the handle of the car door to restrain myself from running for the elevator.

Then there is the insanity of driving at high speed, trying to beat the yellow light or weaving in and out of traffic, risking injury to oneself and others, all to gain a minute or two. The lack of patience is certainly evident in "road rage," and people have been known to physically attack or even shoot someone who cuts in front of them. This is Spiritual Deficiency Syndrome in the extreme.

There are some situations where seconds may count, as in getting prompt treatment for a heart attack. However, we tend to respond with impatience even when there is no need for immediacy. A common, irritating manifestation of impatience is interrupting other peoples' sentences before they are finished.

Someone once heard a child say, "I is … " and the parent interrupted, saying, "That's wrong. You must say 'I am.'"

The child shrugged. "Okay. I *am* the ninth letter of the alphabet."

I once came across an advertisement for a very expensive automobile, whose merits were announced in bold letters: "0 to 60 MPH in 6.3 seconds." This aroused my curiosity. One day, on an empty highway, I tested my car. It took all of twelve seconds to reach 60 MPH. I couldn't understand why someone would pay $40,000 more for 5.7 seconds. Furthermore, I wondered, just where would someone utilize this technological miracle?

Our current cultural obsession and preoccupation with speed is surely a symptom of Spiritual Deficiency Syndrome and, instead of getting us more quickly to happiness, is literally a roadblock to it. Charles Schulz, creator of the *Peanuts* comic strip, captured this cultural ethos in the following cartoon:

Where we are going seems to be secondary. What seems to be important is that we be the first one *somewhere*. However, many people seem
to be in great haste to get *nowhere*. Patience is not only essential for
self-fulfillment but also for physical, mental, and spiritual health.

Good for the Body

An upholsterer who was refurbishing the chairs in the waiting room
of a cardiology office asked, "What kind of doctors are you?"

One of the cardiologists said, "We are heart doctors. Why do you ask?"

"It's a funny thing," the upholsterer said, "your chairs are worn
out only at the very front."

Looking at the chairs, the doctors realized that their patients did
not sit back on the full chair. Rather, they sat on the very edge of the
chair, ready to jump up the moment they were called. This might not
have been so impressive if not for the fact that many had to wait for an
hour or more for the doctor, *yet the entire time, they sat on the very edge
of the chair.*

Drs. Friedman and Rosenman then began their investigation
about personality types that were particularly vulnerable to develop
heart disease. They found that the major features of what they termed
"Type A Personality" were that these people were always on the move,
had a strong sense of urgency, operated under pressure of time,
checked their watches more frequently, and were very irritable and
impatient with anyone or anything that interfered with what they
were doing.

In other words, being impatient is tough on the human body!
Who knows how much healthier we could be if we increased our ability to practice patience.

Patience can even, literally, save your life. You're reclining on the
couch, and the phone rings. You jump up to answer the phone, and
you feel dizzy, grabbing onto something to keep from falling. Here's
what happened: while you were lying down, your heart was pumping

blood to your head horizontally. When you jumped up, your heart had to pump against gravity, and your brain was momentarily deprived of blood. This can even cause a mini-stroke. Being patient and getting up slowly—allowing the phone to ring a few more times—can be life-saving!

Good for the Mind

Technology has developed wonderful mechanisms. Not-so-wonderful mechanisms are the recorded messages, "Press 1 ..." and various numbers after that, and finally, "Please hold for the next available agent." Think of Susan, who was trying to wrap up some things at the office in order to make a flight. When she called to check the departure time, she slammed down the receiver after pushing more numbers than she could count and waiting three long minutes. If she had waited just a bit longer, she would have found out that her flight had been delayed two hours. Patience would have given her some much-needed time to complete her work and would have reduced the stress on her overloaded mind.

Our minds have been programmed since childhood to respond in certain ways, and if something sets a program in action, we may respond automatically and later regret it. For example, if an overly strict parent has sensitized you to criticism, any criticism may trigger an anger response. If your employer criticizes you, your automatic response may cost you your job. If you develop patience, you can delay a response until you can think through whether or not it is wise. It is hard to gain mental clarity under pressure. Patience, on the other hand, allows your internal wisdom time to come to the surface.

Good for the Spirit

I was late for my dental appointment. As I drove into the multilevel parking lot, there were two cars ahead of me looking for a parking space, and the lead car was crawling at a snail's pace. The guy in front of me was blasting his horn, and I was tempted to do likewise to get the lead car to move on. However, I reasoned that there was no need to add to the cacophony. As the lead car swung around the corner, I noticed the handicap symbol on the license plate. I was so happy that I was patient enough not to add to that driver's misery.

There is truth in the aphorism "Haste makes waste." We may discover that, had we been more patient, we would have gotten a better deal. Far more important than a better deal is that, by being patient, we will not have to regret having said words that we cannot retrieve. Knee-jerk reactions may offend others. The spirituality of being patient is very beneficial to the condition of our spirit and a key to our level of happiness.

7

The Ability to
Make the Most of
Circumstances

*B*eing *the best we can be* may vary with time and circumstances. When we're twenty-five, we need to be the best we can be at age twenty-five. When we're seventy-five, we need to be the best we can be at age seventy-five.

A New Expectation

The Talmud relates an enlightening incident. The great sage Rabbi Eliezer fell seriously ill, and several of his disciples visited him. Each one expressed his gratitude for the priceless teaching the rabbi had provided, making statements such as, "Our Master, you have been better for us than the sun and the rain, because they only provide for us in this earthly world, whereas, you, Master, have provided us with sustenance unto eternity."

Rabbi Eliezer did not acknowledge any of them.

Then one disciple, Rabbi Akiva, said, "Suffering, too, can be precious."

At this point the great sage said, "Help me sit up so that I can better hear what my dear student, Akiva, is saying."

Why did the sage ignore the other disciples and respond only to this one?

As a spiritual person, Rabbi Eliezer did not rest on his laurels. He did not focus on the accomplishments of the past. Rather, he was constantly seeking to fulfill himself. Therefore, the accolades about his past performance meant little to him. He was concerned about what he could do now, and in his frail condition, he realized he was unable to do anything. The last disciple had reminded him that self-fulfillment is dependent on our capacities *at any given point in time*. If we can do little, but we do it wholly, we have a better chance at happiness than the person who can do much but, instead, does little. The happiness that comes with fulfilling ourselves—even if by objective measurements we have done less than a more-gifted person—has little to do with comparative measurements.

The opposite is true as well: if we have done *more* than a less-gifted person, but have not done it wholly, we will not be fulfilled. I am reminded of the composer Gioacchina Rossini, whose musical compositions, operas, and overtures are enchantingly beautiful. Tradition has it that Rossini stopped composing music at age thirty-five, and for the next forty-one years of his life wrote nothing simply because he was lazy. If this is true, then Rossini was grossly unfulfilled, having denied his extraordinary talent. A composer who wrote much less music but gave fully whatever he had to give would have been more fulfilled than Rossini—and much happier.

The disciple's wise words to the sage spoke volumes about finding human happiness, even in the midst of reduced circumstances. "During the years that you were capable of teaching, that was your obligation and your assignment in life, and at that point you were fulfilling yourself by teaching. In your present condition, you are unable to do that. If all you can do now is accept your suffering with equanimity, without anger and rancor, and you do that, then you are doing all that you can, and that is all that can be expected of anyone."

A New Yardstick

If you have ever been in acute pain, you know what I mean when I say, "The whole world shrinks." If you have a very bad toothache or the excruciating pain of stubbing a toe, you are aware of only one thing: your tooth or your toe, and you want relief. Only when the pain is gone can you get back to normal life. But, typically, short-term acute pain does not have much impact on self-fulfillment.

It is different, however, when the pain is chronic or when people are disabled, such as by a stroke, multiple sclerosis, or any other condition that severely restricts people's abilities to function. At such times, there may be a sharp decrease in self-esteem. The inability to function normally, especially if there does not seem to be any light at the end of the tunnel, can cause people to feel that self-fulfillment and happiness have become impossibilities.

I once made a pastoral call to a young woman who suffered from a debilitating form of multiple sclerosis. In a very short period of time, she had lost all motor function as well as her vision. She was bedfast and could not attend to her personal needs. She could not see her two young children, who had actually become afraid of approaching her. She asked me, "Rabbi, why am I alive? What purpose is there to my existence?"

I shared the Talmudic story of Rabbi Eliezer with this young woman. While it certainly did not relieve her agony over her tragic condition, she realized that there was something she could do, even in her totally disabled state.

People disabled by illness are not the only ones who may feel unproductive and, therefore, of lesser value. Similar feelings may occur when people lose their jobs, or their marriage breaks up, or their financial circumstances change: they not only lose their "position" but their self-esteem as well.

The value of a person cannot be measured by the commercial yardstick of profit and loss. Happiness has no correlation with the industrial concept of productivity. The measure of our happiness lies in our self-fulfillment, in being the best we can be, *even*—maybe *especially*—in tough circumstances. Being able to analyze our present circumstances and develop "a new yardstick" for the measurement of our value is the key to our pursuit of happiness.

A New Appreciation

In the last half-century, we have been the beneficiaries of a boom in medical science that has doubled the average life expectancy. However, many of the wear-and-tear diseases of later life, especially mental impairment, have not been conquered. This means that we will have an ever-increasing population of people who live past their productive years. Unless we understand that we all have value in self-fulfillment, a large segment of the population will suffer from Spiritual Deficiency Syndrome of chronic discontent.

In a workshop for health professionals who provide home care, a nurse complained about her frustration with one elderly client who was always critical of whatever anyone did for her. "Why have you come so late? I've been waiting for you for almost an hour," she would accuse the nurse. Or, "The blood pressure cuff is too tight. You're hurting me." Or, "You've confused me about taking my medication. Now I don't know what to do." Or, "The bath water is too cool (or too hot)."

"She is critical about everything I do," the nurse bemoaned. "Forget about saying, 'Thank you'!"

This reminded me of an incident when I was an intern and was called to administer an intravenous antibiotic to a patient. This patient happened to be an octogenarian who had been a member of my father's congregation. She had known me from my infancy and had frequently visited our home. Now she was a bilateral-leg amputee and was hospitalized because of pneumonia.

As I was about to give her the injection, I said, "This is only going to be a tiny pinch, Grandma. It won't hurt much."

"Foolish child," she said. "Let it hurt. Do you think anyone wants to leave a world that is pleasant?"

This helped me understand why some elderly people may be cantankerous. I think about it like this: if the last two days of my vacation are bright and sunny, going back to the office may be an ordeal. If the last two days are cold and rainy, it is much easier to return home.

Elderly people know, consciously or subconsciously, that their time is running out. It is much easier to accept life coming to an end if living is unpleasant. That, in turn, is why they may make life appear to be miserable.

I said to the nurse, "I'm sure that your patient really does appreciate what you do for her, but she has to complain about everything. By making the world appear inhospitable, it is easier for her to accept the inevitable."

"By the way," I added, "what is the very last thing this woman says to you when you are about to leave?"

"She asks, 'When are you coming back?'" the nurse said.

"See?" I said. "She *does* appreciate you. She just can't admit it."

Self-fulfillment for the elderly may look very different from self-fulfillment for younger people. Yet the concept of being the best we can be, in whatever condition or circumstances we are in, applies universally. It is not enough for just the ill or elderly to accept this. Acceptance is a spiritual concept and is a key component of self-fulfillment and happiness.

8

The Ability to
Improve

If you have a small automobile that has a four-cylinder engine that can generate say, 60 horsepower, you may not be able to burn up the road, but you will reach your destination with a fairly comfortable ride. On the other hand, if you have an automobile with a powerful V-8 engine that can generate 300 horsepower, but two of the eight cylinders are not functioning, you may have a very uncomfortable ride. Although the six functioning cylinders may generate 200 horsepower (more than three times that of the smaller engine!), the ride will not be smooth. The nonfunctioning cylinders may cause the car to vibrate. Of course, the engine cannot feel anything. It is you, the passenger, who will be uncomfortable.

Four-Cylinder vs. Eight-Cylinder People

Some people are "four-cylinder" people: they have limited endowment. Then there are "eight-cylinder" people who have much greater potential. If the latter do not try to exercise all of their eight cylinders, they will be less happy than the four-cylinder people, who, though they might do and achieve less, are likely to be content because they are using all their cylinders.

Here's a case that illustrates my point.

Stephen was a very bright law student who fulfilled the class prediction that he would be the most likely to succeed. He developed a law firm with a staff of forty-two lawyers and represented a number of major corporations. He was proud of his home and his Jaguar.

Stephen's wife complained that he had no time for her or their children because he often worked late hours at the office. "He lives for the firm, not for us," she would say. His wife was active in a number of community organizations, but he ridiculed her participation. His charity was essentially limited to the mandatory gift to United Way.

Stephen's son, Barry, entered law school and did well. At the end of his second year, however, he shocked his parents by declaring that he was dropping out of law school. Convinced that the young man must be having a mental crisis, they sent him to me for a psychiatric evaluation.

Barry was pleasant and completely coherent and appropriate in the interview. He denied feeling depressed. He said that, while initially he had wanted to follow in his father's footsteps, he had begun rethinking this in the beginning of the second year.

"I know I could be a good lawyer," Barry said, "but I don't want to emulate my father. I respect him for his brilliance and accomplishments, but I don't see being the head of a large law firm as my goal in life. I love my father, so I hate to say this, but all he is is a lawyer, not really a person. I am not a particularly religious person, but I don't think that people are created only to perform at work. There has got to be something more to life.

"My dad is not a happy man. His preoccupation with the firm is his escape. Many of his cohorts drink heavily, but he doesn't—the firm is his alcohol. Even when we're on vacation, he is in constant contact with the office. The office doesn't need him, he needs the office. I don't want to end up feeling miserable like my dad, looking for some kind of escape.

"I'm not sure what I'll do. I may even decide to go back to law school in the future, if they'll take me. Right now, I want to take some time off to find out what life is really all about—and what I am all about. I have to find a goal that makes sense for me."

I could not detect any pathology in Barry. He was not unrealistic; he had no desire to become a beachcomber. He knew that he had to have a career and did not dismiss law as a possibility. But he thirsted for something more in his life than his dad had found. Barry's search was leading him in the direction of happiness.

Our personality cylinders are the various human potentials. These include not only our innate talents and skills, but also our potential to be spiritual. Stephen escaped from the discomfort of the unused spiritual cylinder by indulging in work. Barry was more fortunate, sensing that happiness requires functioning with all his cylinders, and he ventured out to find the missing cylinder.

Ambition vs. Proving Yourself

If we are doing many good things, that contributes to being *the best person we can be*, right? Yes ... but not always. Ironically, people who seem to be doing a lot of good may actually be detracting from self-fulfillment and spirituality. The distinction lies in whether they are seeking approval or following their ambition.

An ambitious person does things because she has the ability to do them, wants to do them, and enjoys doing them. A classic example of this is the nursing mother, who feels uncomfortable until the infant nurses, which relieves her discomfort. Several hours later, when her milk supply has been replenished, she again feels discomfort. She wishes to give to the infant because she has the nourishment to give and is uncomfortable if the infant does not take it from her.

Another example is a teacher who enjoys sharing his knowledge with his students. The more questions they ask, the more he is stimulated to teach. I can recall teachers who probably would have taught even without a salary, if it were not for the need to support a family. They taught because they loved to teach.

People who have solid self-esteem, and do things because they wish to share what they have, invariably enjoy what they are doing. Their actions give them a feeling of satisfaction; they are aware of their abilities and fulfill them. This strengthens their character and makes them better people. Such people are *ambitious*.

On the other hand, people who have unwarranted feelings of inferiority may be distressed because they have a constant need to be validated by others. Without continual recognition, they feel unworthy. They may be engaged in a number of community projects, and when their efforts are appreciated, they have a momentary sense of worthiness. However, because their feelings of inferiority have no basis in fact, their feelings of unworthiness are essentially delusions, and *delusions are never refuted by reality*. An anorexic young woman who weighs sixty pounds may have the delusion that she is fat. When she loses another half-pound, she may feel better for a short while, only to decide that she must lose more weight. There is no satisfying a delusion.

A prominent industrialist who suffered from peptic ulcer disease said, "In my home I have a whole wall covered with honorary plaques, tributes, and trophies. They don't mean anything to me." The recognition and honors bestowed upon him did not have a lasting effect. Here was an excellent person who did not believe in himself, and all his efforts at trying to prove himself, while greatly benefiting the community, were futile in giving him self-esteem.

Trying to prove ourselves is essentially a psychological defense in an attempt to ward off feelings of unworthiness and inferiority. It is normal to wish to be appreciated. However, if we do things for other people only because we seek their affection and approval, we are "people junkies," totally dependent on others' opinions. There is no way we can be genuine—or happy—because we will always need to be changing our behavior to comply with what we think others want. In the attempt to satisfy everyone, we will exhaust ourselves.

The cartoonist Charles Schulz depicts this in his inimitable way:

Snoopy wants to please both girls, so he droops one side of his face to satisfy the girl who likes a dog with a sad expression, and he elevates the other side to please the girl who prefers a cheerful expression. But rather than achieving his goal of pleasing both, Snoopy is actually disappointing both of them. His happy expression is disappointing to the former girl, and his sad expression is disappointing to the latter. Furthermore, since it requires great effort to maintain both postures simultaneously, Snoopy is exhausting himself in a futile effort to please everyone.

I can identify with people who crave recognition. When I was a newly ordained rabbi, I assumed the position as assistant to my father in his congregation. My father was an illustrious person who had become a legend in his lifetime. Although I was proud to be his son, I felt pain whenever I was introduced as "Rabbi Twerski's son." I wanted to be my own person.

One day I was visiting one of our congregants who had undergone surgery, and she said to me, "It was truly amazing. Nothing they were giving me relieved my pain, but when your father walked in, the pain disappeared, as if by magic."

I left the hospital room knowing that I could not stand in my father's shadow. This was crushing to my self-esteem. I had been doing a number of things to impress people with my importance.

This was the beginning of my decision to leave the rabbinate for a career in medicine.

Shifting from proving ourselves to fulfilling ourselves is not an overnight occurrence; for most of us, it is a lifetime journey. I once gave several lectures to a group of addiction therapists. A few weeks later, I received a packet of 110 evaluations of my lectures. Of these, *109* were glowingly flattering, but I was crushed by the lone negative evaluation. Because I felt I needed to "prove myself," I was extremely sensitive to the criticism. For three weeks, I suffered from depression, until it occurred to me that 109 to 1 is quite a favorable score.

People who seek to gain recognition by proving themselves and receiving praise may become overachievers. What they accomplish may be very constructive, but the recognition and approval they continually seek will come at an inordinate cost to them and their families. They will suffer from chronic Spiritual Deficiency Syndrome, and happiness will be fleeting, at best.

Ambition is self-fulfilling, but proving ourselves is not.

Self-Fulfillment vs. Perfectionism

It is not uncommon for people to feel that, unless they achieve perfection, they are not fulfilled. The mistake in this is that they are striving for self-fulfillment as a god or some kind of angel, rather than as a *human being*. It is important that we be as aware of our limitations as our potential.

No human being goes through life without experiencing some failures. While failures are unpleasant, they do not need to be catastrophic unless we make them so. The aphorism that "Experience is a hard teacher, but fools learn no other way" is utterly wrong. It is the wise who learn from experience. Fools do not learn from their mistakes.

There is no end point to the character growth of which we human beings are capable. All of the traits that are unique to humans are capable of infinite improvement. Striving to be the best we can be is healthy—whether as a pianist, scientist, or human being. However, it should not be confused with perfectionism—the latter is a costly trait.

Perfectionism is often the result of low self-esteem. People with solid self-esteem will not be shattered by a failure, whereas people with poor self-esteem dread a failure because it confirms their worst fears about themselves.

Perfectionists are apt to behave in one of three ways:

- They avoid trying to do anything. If they don't try, they cannot fail. Obviously, with no effort, there can be no results, so these perfectionists are always disappointed in themselves.
- They make sure that what they do is perfect. Because perfection is not within human capability, these perfectionists frequently feel like failures and are depressed.
- They set themselves up for failure. If perfectionists undertake a venture and fear it may fail, they may sabotage it and precipitate the failure, simply to be free of the extreme tension of *anticipating* a failure. The self-imposed failure will reduce their self-esteem every time.

Take the case of Herbert. He had graduated with an accounting degree but was turned down on his first job application. Thereafter, he would not get out of bed until late in the day, and he made all kinds of excuses about why he could not look for a job. The fact was, he was afraid of another rejection, which he saw as a failure and could not tolerate. Although by not applying for a job, he was failing, it was easier for him to tolerate a passive failure than the active failure of being rejected.

Then there was Evelyn. She was so afraid of making a mistake at work that she spent hours, instead of a few minutes, with each microscopic tissue slide before making a diagnosis. Within a month at her position, she was three weeks behind and was dismissed.

When perfectionism is carried to an extreme to protect low self-esteem, it can be counterproductive. When I get on a plane, I want the pilot to check all the indicators on the instrument panel to make sure that the aircraft can operate properly, but if the pilot is excessively perfectionistic and rechecks each dial numerous times, the plane may never take off.

Spiritual people understand the need to continually be improving themselves and be the best they can be, but they do not confuse this with perfection. They know that, along the way, they will experience setbacks, but these do not discourage them from continuing to strive for self-improvement.

The great piano virtuoso Vladimir Horowitz used to practice playing the piano several hours every day. He was always improving his ability. Then there was the actress who, on the last day of a Broadway show that ran for three years, excitedly said that she had thought of a better way to say her lines. When someone pointed out to her that the show was closing, she said, "But there is still tonight."

We can always be improving ourselves. But our happiness lies in becoming *better*—not in trying to be perfect.

9

The Ability to Be Compassionate

Being self-aware, humble, purposeful in our choices, patient, and on the path to self-improvement are all important ingredients for happiness, but they are not enough. Unlike animals who are totally motivated by self-gratification, we human beings have the ability to look beyond our personal needs and do things for others.

Compassion is the unique human ability to care about other people, to be considerate of others and sensitive to their needs. We can even help people whom we do not know, people who are total strangers, thanks to one of the unique components of the human spirit: the ability to empathize. We can identify with people in need, and knowing how we would appreciate help, we can provide help for them.

Compassionate Empathy

Do animals feel joy? After their stomachs are full, they act as though they are quite content, and we humans, too, can feel content when our hunger is abated. However, this is not quite the same as feeling joy. Even the elation of winning a jackpot is not the unique human feeling of joy. It is merely another instance of satisfying the acquisitive drive, which is present in animals as well.

There are feelings of joy that are rather unique to human beings, such as the joy of achievement, of completing a difficult task, of making a new discovery, or of celebrating the success of others. Many of us experienced joy when we saw Neil Armstrong take his first step on the moon … and we felt profound sorrow when the Discovery space flight exploded in midair. Animals probably also feel something like sadness when they are hurt or experience a loss, but that is not the same as the grief that human beings can feel.

A while back, several coal miners were trapped hundreds of feet below the surface of the Earth, certain to die if they could not be reached in time. People sat with their eyes glued to the television, watching the rescue efforts and feeling the anguish of the miners' wives and families. When each miner was brought out of the mine, there were shouts of joy by people who were hundreds of miles away, sharing the relief of that miner's family, while still feeling the agony of those whose loved ones continued to be in great danger. When the last of the trapped miners was rescued, the joy was felt by everyone from coast to coast. People hugged each other in jubilation.

These miners and their families were strangers to many of us, but this did not prevent us from sharing their feelings. This was a spiritual experience. The ability to share others' joy or grief is uniquely human, a significant component of the human spirit.

We generally do not have much difficulty in sharing the joy of others, but we may guard ourselves from feeling their pain. In my early days as a rabbi, I had the distressing experience of officiating at the funeral of a three-year-old child who had drowned. The following day, I made a condolence call and found a number of family members and close friends sitting together. One by one, each person left the room, and I was left alone with the mother, who cried out her bitter heart. I listened to her but could not find anything to say that might be comforting. The next day, the scene was repeated. Everyone left the room, and the mother cried to me. This went on for several days.

Then I received a phone call from the mother's parents, thanking me for what I was doing for Beverly. I was perplexed. I wasn't doing *anything* for Beverly! I had not been able to think of anything to say to relieve her grief.

But eventually I understood what was happening. Beverly's family and close friends were so personally affected by this terrible tragedy that they could not listen to Beverly's expression of pain. They were suffering too much to be present to her grief. Instead, they would make conversation about any other subject to avoid touching on the tragedy. When I came in, everyone would leave the room, and only then would Beverly have the opportunity to cry and to release her grief. True, I had nothing to say, but *I was able to listen*, and that provided a modicum of comfort.

Sometimes I am asked whether my having been a rabbi has had any effect on my practice as a physician. I think it has. As a physician, I try to *fix* people's pain, to relieve them of their suffering. But as a rabbi, I learned to *share* people's pain. As advanced as modern medicine is, there are still times when I cannot fix things, but I can always share.

I can attest to this from personal experience. When my wife died, friends visited me, and when we spoke about my wife, I would cry. I began to notice that some friends stopped visiting me. Evidently, they felt awkward seeing me cry and about not being able to say anything comforting, so they simply avoided me. But I needed to cry, and it was not enough to cry by myself. I needed someone to feel along with me.

Since I often attended meetings of recovering alcoholics, I began asking whether any of the attendees could spare a few moments after the meeting. Four or five people generally stayed on, and I would talk to them about my loss, and cry. No one got up and left. They were willing to listen to me and to absorb my pain. Their experience in recovering from alcoholism had made them emotionally receptive. They were not frightened away by my crying. They listened with great empathy, and that was just what I needed.

Sometimes, we are privileged to be of actual help to people who are grieving. But even when there is nothing we can do to help people, we can feel *for* them and *with* them. That, too, is a form of help. It has been said that "joy shared is doubled, and sorrow shared is halved." Empathizing with people and sharing their feelings is a unique, spiritual human trait. Whether the feelings shared are joy or grief, the fulfillment of the sharing itself is a source of true happiness.

Compassionate Parenting

Compassion can be a biological trait, as can be seen in the maternal care of animals for their young. Animals teach their young how to look for food and how to avoid predators. Mother bears teach their cubs how to look for food, and when the cubs are able to fend for themselves, the mother bear leads them into the forest and takes off, essentially abandoning them. Nature has provided a maternal instinct that, in the end, helps the cubs to become self-sufficient. Animal parenting is for survival, nothing more.

Parental compassion is present in the biology of humans as well. Parents may make many sacrifices for their children and even give away their lives to preserve their child's life. This is certainly a heartwarming trait, but since it is of biological nature and is present in animals as well, it is not a component of spirituality. As wonderful as parental love for a child may be, it does not necessarily lead to self-fulfillment and happiness as a human being.

There is, however, a parental compassion that is uniquely human, a compassion that is spiritual. When parents give priority time to take a serious interest in a child's life, and enable that child to become the best person he or she can be, that is spiritual compassion.

If a busy parent tells me, "I would love to spend more time with my children, but I just don't have the time, my office is virtually a 24/7 operation," I tell the parent the following anecdote.

A man drove up to a motel that had a "No Vacancy" sign and asked for a room. The clerk said, "Didn't you see the 'No Vacancy' sign? We're full."

The man said, "You mean to tell me that if the President of the United States were to come here, you would not have a room for him?"

The clerk replied, "Well, we would have to do something to accommodate the President."

"Good!" the man said. "The President is not coming. You can give me his room."

Similarly, we need to make "room" for our children, even though economic pressures demand much of our time. Parents who do not spend time with their children—even if that time away from their children allows them to earn more money to provide for their children's wants and needs—are sending a subtle nonverbal message: "What I can buy for you is more important than what I can give you, of myself, as a parent." I have never heard people in the last days of their lives say, "My one regret is that I did not spend more time at the office." Their regret is invariably for not having spent more time with the family.

A key factor in compassionate parenting is providing a listening ear for children. Did you know that a research study, in which hundreds of families were interviewed and numerous details were recorded, concluded that the most outstanding characteristic of no-children-problem families was *the frequency with which the family shared meals together*? The research found that the family mealtime created a sense of belonging and allowed parents to remain aware of what was going on with their children. (Incidentally, the children in the frequent-mealtime-together families developed more extensive vocabularies at an early age and scored two to three grade levels higher on standardized reading and language tests.)*

Just as spirituality means *being the best person we can be*, so, too, does spiritual parenting mean helping children become *the best they can be*. And that means listening with our full attention so we can

---

* Bowden, B., and Zeisz, J. "Family Meals May Prevent Teen Problems." *APA Monitor*, 28 (10): 8 Oct., 1997.

understand our children and recognize the unique ways in which each child is endowed. Only then will we be able to help our children maximize their uniqueness.

I know a family in which both parents are intellectuals, and one of their sons follows in their footsteps. They are very proud of this son. The other son is below average academically and is bored to death by school. However, he is a mechanical genius. He loves to tinker with things, and he can take apart and reassemble the most complex machine. The parents are distraught that he has no desire to excel academically, and they do not conceal their disappointment in him.

This is not spiritual parenting because their goal for their children is what pleases them rather than what is optimum for the child. Just as adults need to be self-fulfilled to be happy, so do children.

Compassionate Marriage

Our culture is awash in love. From soap operas to movies, to a plethora of magazines and books, love is a dominant theme. Yet, we are told that *more than half of all marriages today end in divorce.* Something is clearly wrong. Why do so many marriages fail, resulting in misery for both spouses and profound emotional trauma for their children? The emotional wreckage resulting from divorce is alarming, and the statistics that one out of three children in the United States lives in a single-parent home does not bode well for the mental health of our society.

Perhaps this anecdote sheds some light.

Rabbi Mendel of Kotzk once came across a young man who was obviously enjoying a dish of fish.

"Why are you eating the fish?" the rabbi asked.

The young man answered, "Because I love fish."

"And so," the rabbi said, "because of your love for the fish, you took it out of the water, killed it, and cooked it. I dare say that is a strange kind of love.

"You see, young man," the rabbi continued, "you say that you love the fish, but the truth is that you really do not love the fish at all. It is *yourself* that you love, and because the taste of fish pleases your palate, you killed it to satisfy your appetite."

What often passes for "love" in modern society is very often "fish love." When two people "fall in love," it is usually because the man sees in the woman someone he feels can provide for *his* physical and emotional needs, and she sees in the man someone she thinks can provide for *her* physical and emotional needs. While they each think they love the other person, it is really *themselves* they love. He wants *his* needs satisfied, and she wants *her* needs satisfied.

George Bernard Shaw once said, "When two people are under the influence of the most violent, most insane, most illusive, and most transient of passions, they are required to swear that they will remain in that excited, abnormal, and exhausting condition continuously until death do them part."

That is *not* what marriage vows are meant to be, and it is this misunderstanding of marriage vows that results in disillusionment. It is understandable that a marriage may begin with physical and emotional attraction. However, it needs to grow and mature into something much more compatible with the dignity and uniqueness of a human being. In a spiritual marriage, each partner wants to maximize the *other* partner's happiness rather than his or her own.

There are such marriages. I was fortunate to witness one: my parents' marriage.

Although not a physician, my father had an extensive knowledge of medicine. As a rabbi, he made daily visits to hospitalized patients, and over the years of discussing their cases with the doctors, he acquired a fair amount of medical information. When he developed cancer of the pancreas with involvement of the liver, he said to me, "Chemotherapy doesn't do anything for pancreatic cancer, does it?"

I replied that it did not.

"Then there is no point in suffering all the side effects of chemotherapy if it cannot do any good, is there?"

I had to agree that he was right, and I concurred with his decision not to have chemotherapy.

However, the doctor told my mother, "There's not much we can do for the rabbi. At best, chemotherapy can get us three more months."

My mother told my father, "Three months? Why, it would be worth it for even three *days*! Every single day is precious!" She insisted, in no uncertain terms, that he undergo chemotherapy.

After my mother left the room, my father said to me, "I'm sorry that the doctor gave Mother the wrong information. I know that it will not extend my life for three months. But if I refuse chemotherapy, then when I die, Mother will say, 'Why didn't I insist on it? If I had insisted on it, he would still be alive,' and she will feel guilty for not insisting. I don't want her to feel guilty. So I will take chemotherapy."

My father paused, then added, "I've done many things for Mother during our fifty-two years. This gives me a chance to do one last thing."

Theirs was a spiritual marriage.

True love is *self-fulfilling*, rather than *selfish*. True love is consideration for another person and doing the utmost to make the other person happier. True love is uniquely human.

Compassionate Relationships

If compassion means relating to people by understanding them, empathizing with them, and being sensitive to their needs, then trying to control people is surely the polar opposite. Control by power is an animal trait observed in many species (the pecking order) when one animal rises to the top and becomes a dictator before whom the other animals cower.

Exerting control over other people is particularly tragic because it is extremely counterproductive. But we humans are very vulnerable to this flaw, particularly in husband-wife and parent-child relationships. Whether the control is by physical force, through verbal threats, or by withholding money or affection, control is control. People who are experiencing chronic discontent because of lack of self-fulfillment may try to achieve a feeling of importance by exercising control over other people. If people quake before them and follow their orders, it may make them feel they are "somebody," and they may mistakenly feel self-fulfilled.

People who fulfill themselves by controlling others are caught in a vicious cycle. Because control is the antithesis of true self-fulfillment, the more we try to exert control, the *less* we fulfill ourselves, the greater our symptoms of Spiritual Deficiency Syndrome.

If, say, a parent is provoked into rage and loses control of his or her anger, the parent should subsequently say to the child, "I'm sorry I lost it. Yes, I was very angry, but I did not have to scream and carry on like I did. I'm going to try hard to control my anger, so that I do not explode like that." This is a powerful lesson of spirituality and self-fulfillment.

One father related his experience: "Last week I was at the breakfast table with my four-year-old son, Pete. Pete trusts me, and I love him with every fiber of my being. But that morning I was not on my game. He did something, and I snapped at him. I told him to stop being bad, sit up straight, and be a good boy.

"The look in his eyes about killed me. I had betrayed him in a way he had never thought possible. In a second, he ran from the table and hid in his room.

"I went to Pete's room, took his hands in mine, and told him how sorry I was. I told him Daddy sometimes doesn't feel just right and makes mistakes. I told him Daddy was probably going to be crying in a minute, but that was okay because tears sometimes happen when you feel sad about something.

"Then Pete turned the table on who was holding whose hands. He held mine and said, 'Daddy, I'm feeling something deep.' I asked him what it was. He said he didn't know the name of the feeling. But he crawled up inside my arms and put his face right against mine. He was crying, too. We stayed like that a long time."

Father and son both had a spiritual experience. Their ability to feel empathy for each other was more powerful than any need for control. By being truly sensitive to his son's needs, the father not only earned his son's love and respect, but he was also being the best father he could be—mistakes and all—which brought him the happiness he truly desired with his son.

I'll share one last story that makes the point about the link between compassion and spirituality better than any more words I could add.

In Lexington, Massachusetts, December 1995, a windblown fire destroyed Malden Mills, effectively stealing Christmas from its fourteen hundred workers. Malden Mills was the only game in town. Obviously, seventy-year-old Aaron Feuerstein, the mill's owner, would simply retire and close down the mill.

Feuerstein remembered his father's teaching: "In a situation that is devoid of morality, try to be thoughtful and do something worthwhile." Feuerstein met with the workers and told them he would keep them all on full payroll with full benefits for at least a month, during which he would make every effort to reopen the mill.

The word spread, and donations poured in from all over the country: money, toys for the children, frozen turkeys, and even tickets to the performance of the *Nutcracker Suite* in nearby Boston.

These were all spiritual people. I'm sure that all the donors truly enjoyed their Christmas dinners that year.

That is another feature of compassion: it is contagious.

10

The Ability to
Have Perspective

Shortly after my son's marriage, the newlyweds visited us for a weekend. When they were preparing to return home, they could not find their return flight tickets. They went through all their suitcases and every piece of clothing. We conducted a thorough search of all the rooms, but to no avail. The tickets had somehow disappeared.

This was a calamity! The advance-purchase fare for their weekend trip had been low, but the price of two "same-day" tickets was an astronomical sum, an intolerable expenditure for a young couple. To say that they were extremely aggravated is a gross understatement.

Twenty-one years later, as my son escorted his oldest child to the wedding canopy, I asked him, "Do you remember the lost tickets? Was it really the catastrophe you made it out to be?" He smiled.

We may not be able to foresee the future, but we can recognize that what seems to be mountains at the present might be molehills in retrospect. We may be able to recall experiences that seemed dreadful at the time they occurred, but, put into perspective, they turned out to be insignificant or even blessings in disguise.

The ability to have perspective—to see things as they really were, or to see things as they might be—is one of the unique spiritual traits that we humans have. We can review the past, think about consequences of our actions, and contemplate the future.

Perspective of the Future

While animals may instinctively store food for the future, as do squirrels, who hoard food for the winter, it is unlikely that animals can contemplate the future, plan for it, and think about the future consequences of their actions. Serious consideration of the future, particularly the consequences of our actions, is a spiritual, human trait.

A classic example of this is addicts who are fully aware that their addiction may be harmful. Though they love life and want to have a healthy future, they are essentially willing to risk everything for the transient pleasant sensation of their addiction. This is the classic behavior of compulsive gamblers or addicts who live for the pleasure of the moment, not considering the deleterious consequences. But many characteristics of addiction can be found in nonaddicts, only in a more subtle form. When we have a strong desire for something, we may ignore the consequences of satisfying that desire. Even after experiencing the negative effects of a particular behavior, we may still repeat the behavior, with total disregard for logical thinking. It has been said, for good reason, that insanity is *repeating the same act but expecting different results.*

Collectively, we are grossly derelict in this aspect of humanity, sometimes behaving as if there were no future, for example, in our treatment of our planet. We destroy the forests, pollute the air and water, and exhaust resources of energy as though they were infinite. We respect the knowledge of scientists, and although we may not doubt the validity of their predictions, we ignore the phenomena of global warming and the rarefaction of the ozone layer.

The psychological defense of denial may be partially responsible. I was once invited to participate in teaching a course for people between the ages of forty and forty-five to help them plan for their future retirement. We planned to cover financial, physical health, and psychological considerations. We felt this age group was the ideal audience. The course was well publicized, and the program planners were certain there would be standing-room-only attendance. They were shocked and disappointed that attendance was meager.

Squirrels are blessed with an instinct that makes them hoard for the winter. We humans, on the other hand, have to use our intellect to compensate for the absence of instinct. We have to exercise contemplation of our future if we are to be self-fulfilled and happy.

The anticipation of a better future motivates many people. For example, many "get through the workweek" because they can look forward to the weekend. Others look forward to vacation as the salvation of their lives. Yet, with all this emphasis on the future, people may fail to give adequate thought to the future consequences of their actions.

I once attended a scientific convention where the speaker bewailed the paucity of research that is multigenerational, where the results would not be known in the researcher's lifetime. When researchers cannot possibly know the results of their work, they hesitate to commit to the future, and because of this, some important research has never materialized.

While the desire to know the results of a study is understandable, it is nevertheless self-centered. Exercising the commitment to the future is truly spiritual. Because contemplation of the future is a component of the spirit, failure to plan for the future is a symptom of Spiritual Deficiency Syndrome.

How many people do you know who have talked about what they will do "after the kids go off to college" or "after we move into the new house" or "after I get this job" or "after I retire"? One of the hazards of expecting "happiness" in the future is not only that we miss out on happiness today, but that we may also, paradoxically, be denying ourselves happiness in the future!

Take the issue of retirement. Thanks to the remarkable advances of medical science, the average life expectancy in the United States has increased dramatically, from age forty prior to 1940, to eighty in 2007. More people are now living many years after they retire from "work." Some people have financial security, but relatively few people plan adequately for how they will spend their time. Some people assume that once they do not have to punch a time clock, they will be free to do many things they could not do during their working years—play golf, or go fishing to their hearts' content, or travel around the world.

Some people may realize their dreams, but there are many others who may suffer from the wear-and-tear diseases of advanced age, and these conditions may restrict them from doing all the things they had hoped to do. They are then left with the burden of time weighing heavily on their hands. Failure to exercise the spiritual trait of contemplating the future may have deprived them of the happiness to which they had looked forward.

Perspective of the Past

Spirituality involves not only a perspective of the future but also a perspective of the past. While animals know nothing about their ancestors, we human beings have a heritage. We are capable of expanding on the positives of the past and avoiding repetition of historical errors. We can also enjoy the past.

Once, after I had presented a demonstration of hypnosis for a hospital staff, a surgeon approached me. "You must see a patient of mine," he said.

I tried to explain that my schedule was full and that I could not take on any more patients, but the surgeon persisted: "She is a special person who has done many things for the community. She is in pain because of cancer, but she refuses to take pain medication because it clouds her mind and she can't think. I think you can give her pain relief with hypnosis, and you must do it. Frances deserves it."

Frances was brought to the office in a wheelchair. In spite of her pain, she smiled and was pleasant. The first attempt at inducing hypnosis was unsuccessful, which is not unusual. On the second attempt, Frances appeared very relaxed, perhaps in a very shallow hypnotic state. In an effort to deepen the trance, I suggested that she go back in time to any enjoyable occurrence she could remember. After a few minutes, her facial expression indicated that she was indeed enjoying something. I allowed her to dream for a few minutes, then told her to wake up.

"Was that ever fun! I was on a ranch in Wyoming 'doing barrels'," Frances said, explaining that "doing barrels" was a horseback-riding maneuver.

In the next session, Frances dreamt about being on a cruise, and in the next one, she was on the ranch again. However, she was unable to get into a trance that was sufficiently deep to enable pain relief.

On her next visit, she told me that, after reexperiencing one of her vacations on the ranch—a time when they had returned from a day of horseback riding and had had cocoa and marshmallows—she sent her husband to the supermarket for cocoa and marshmallows. Frances had not had an appetite for many weeks.

I called the surgeon to report that the attempt at pain relief was unsuccessful, but before I could say a word, he said, "Dr. Twerski, Bill is so grateful for what you are doing for Frances. She is a new person. She gets around the house without a wheelchair, she hums merry tunes, and she has gone to church for the first time in months."

I was puzzled. It took me a while to realize what was helping Frances.

Most of us live with hopes and anticipation of the future, of pleasant occurrences we can expect: a summer vacation, a promotion at work, graduation, marriage, a new car, or a happy family event. Frances, however, had no pleasant expectations of the future. She knew her disease would take her life within a few months. It was little wonder that she was depressed and that her pain was greatly intensified by her depression.

But now she had something to look forward to. She was excited about what pleasant event she might reexperience in her next hypnosis session, things she could not recall by conscious effort. One time, she remembered being age ten, looking out a window in the loft and imagining that she was queen over the whole land before her. She also recalled many of her activities for the church and for community projects.

Frances taught me that we need not lose the past. It need not be over and done with. Even if we have no pleasant expectations for the future, we can relive the pleasures of the past. Frances lived one year longer than the doctor had expected, and she was happy and active until one week before her death.

A spiritual person can find happiness in both the past and the future.

11

The Ability to
Have Purpose

I do not like fish tanks. I see the fish swimming to and fro, twenty-four hours a day, seven days a week, accomplishing nothing. This makes me think, "Am I really any different? Is it possible that I, too, like the fish, am merely moving about but not really doing anything of true substance? Could an outsider be looking at me and thinking of me what I think of the fish?" Then I wonder: "If these fish can think, is it possible that when they swim to and fro in the tank, they think they *are* accomplishing something?" This is a very uncomfortable thought.

We cannot possibly be happy if we think our existence has no meaning, if we have no goals or aspirations. We each need to find some purpose for our existence.

One of the most unique features of human beings is our ability to contemplate a goal and have a purpose in life. We all need and want to feel valued. But how do we determine value? If we look about us, we see that something has value primarily for one of two reasons: either because it performs a function that we need or, if it is not functional, because it has aesthetic value. We might own a beautiful grandfather clock that, even though the mechanism is broken beyond repair and has no use as a timepiece, we value because it is a handsome piece of furniture. On the other hand, if a can opener becomes dull and cannot open cans, we discard it. Because it has no aesthetic value, it is worthless when it is not functional.

There are some people who are so handsome that they may have an aesthetic value, but they are in the minority. And even these people may eventually lose their aesthetic value in advanced age. Rather, our value as human beings is in our function. But just what is our function? Some put in a full day's work, come home, kick off their shoes, and watch television. Others might spend a few hours at the fitness center working out, or they might meet up with some friends and go out for a delightful dinner. But the truth is, if our lives do not go beyond self-gratification, whatever form that may take, we will continually suffer from signs of Spiritual Deficiency Syndrome. True, a person who enjoys sports or television is more sophisticated than an animal, but even sophisticated self-gratification falls short of the function that can give us a sense of worthiness and self-fulfillment.

Cartoonist Charles Schulz had an uncanny ability to express psychological insights in his cartoons. Below, Schulz humorously depicts how we all need to find some meaning to our life:

Self-fulfillment requires working toward a goal that is more than self-gratification. The human mind, with its stunning capacity, is far too great to settle for only self-gratification. If you saw a boy wearing a jacket whose sleeves extended far beyond his hands, pants that dragged behind him, and a hat that came down over his nose, you would probably conclude that he had put on his father's clothes. Those clothes are far too large for him. Similarly, the abilities that comprise the human spirit are far too great for us to settle for less than the best we can be.

Personal Goals

There is a popular adage, "Where there is a will, there is a way." That saying is obviously not realistic as there are many things we desire that are simply beyond our reach. For example, I have always wanted to conduct a symphony orchestra in Beethoven's Fifth symphony. The only problem is that I cannot read music. I would love to be able to sing operatic arias as Pavarotti does, but alas, I do not have a voice like Pavarotti's, and I never will. It is, therefore, incorrect to say, "Where there is a will, there is a way."

The Talmud expresses this concept a bit differently: "There is nothing that can stand in the way of your will." This does not mean that we can do whatever we wish. Rather, although some things may be impossible for us to do, *there is nothing that can stop us from wanting to do them.* Nothing can stand in the way *of our will.* There is nothing to stop us from dreaming, even if some of our dreams can never be realized. This much is certain: if we do not dream of doing great things, we will never accomplish them.

Great things are accomplished by people who dream of doing them. Although we have our limitations, the fact is that we have enormous untapped energies. There are, for instance, numerous instances where people in crisis have done things that appear to be superhuman. There is a recorded incident of a mother whose baby ran off and crawled underneath a car. In her panic, *the mother raised the car to extract the child.* In her heightened state, her inhibitions were removed, and she was able to do something that four strong people together could not do.

But far beyond any available physical strengths, we have vast amounts of untapped brain power. Neurophysiologists say that we use only a fraction of our brains. It was related that when President Franklin Roosevelt appointed Frank Knox as secretary of the Navy, Roosevelt's aides asked why he had chosen Knox. Roosevelt replied, "He was the only one who did not know that the job could not be done." Unfortunately, we often doubt our abilities, and we resign ourselves to lesser performance because we do not believe we are capable of doing greater things.

In the early 1950s, we witnessed an interesting phenomenon. It was widely accepted that running a four-minute mile was beyond human ability. Then, Roger Bannister broke the record and ran the mile in three minutes fifty-nine seconds. After that, a number of runners did even better. Why hadn't anyone done it earlier? Because everyone had assumed it was impossible.

I once saw a poster depicting birds in flight. The caption read, "They fly because they think they can." Although we might be hesitant to set a high goal for ourselves because we do not want to take the risk of being disappointed with failure, our happiness depends on aspiring to greater things, to being the best we can be.

There is a popular saying, "A horse dreams of a bale of hay." That is all a horse is capable of dreaming of. We can dream of much greater things. True, some of us do not have talents that others have. Some people can see things that others do not see. It is said that when Michelangelo looked at a block of marble, he saw the statue within it. All he had to do was to chip away the exterior marble to reveal it. Though we may lack Michelangelo's extraordinary perception, there is no doubt that we have resources within us that are untapped.

Some people, when passing age fifty or so, may give up on aspiring, figuring that if they have not accomplished anything great until then, they are not likely to do so in their later years. This is a serious mistake. Many great things have been accomplished by people long after they passed the so-called prime of life.

For example, Oscar Hammerstein was sixty-four when he wrote the lyrics to *The Sound of Music*. Michelangelo was seventy-two when he designed the dome of St. Peter's Basilica in Rome. Frank Lloyd Wright was ninety-one when he completed his work on the Guggenheim Museum. In his book *Late Bloomers*, Brendan Gill cites many examples of ordinary people who launched new and productive careers after their retirement.

The key is to think of self-fulfillment in terms of *effort* rather than *outcome*. All we can do is make the best effort possible. The problem is that we have allowed commercial principles to impact our personal lives. In commerce, good and bad are judged by the bottom line. An enterprise that was started in the most careless manner, yet earned a windfall profit, is considered a good business venture. One that was started with careful planning and consultation but went bankrupt is considered a bad business venture. Or think of parents who did their utmost in raising their children but one child turned out to be antisocial. Many would see them as bad parents, while parents who were abusive and neglectful and happened to have a child who was a Nobel Prize winner might be considered good parents.

Spirituality depends on *process* rather than outcome.

Take the example of two surgeons. One surgeon is motivated by avarice and performs a needless operation solely to collect a hefty fee. He happens to find an occult cancer, which was not symptomatic and would not have been detected on any tests. Although he saves the patient's life, he is still a scoundrel.

Another surgeon agonizes about a difficult case. She seeks opinions from several consultants and discusses the high risks with the patient and his family. Ultimately, she concludes that it is in the patient's best interest to operate. Though the patient does not survive the operation, this doctor is honorable and ethical.

If we consider only the results, the first surgeon is good, and the second surgeon is bad. However, the reverse is true. No one has control over outcome, only over process.

Judging by outcome may be appropriate in commerce, but in our personal lives, the measure of success—and, therefore, our happiness—depends on the quality of effort invested. To put it another way, our happiness depends on how and why we do what we do, not on the results. Even if we do not achieve "success" as our commercial world might define it, our efforts will make us *the best persons we can be.*

Family Goals

Just as it is important for each of us to have a goal and a purpose, it is also important that we help our children understand that they, too, have value and meaning and that part of life is finding their own purpose.

A thirty-one-year-old man named Herbert once consulted me with the following problem. "I must have been born under a lucky star because my success in business has been extraordinary. It's not because I'm so bright, I was just an average student. It's that profitable deals just seem to fall into my lap.

"My business requires me to travel in the fast lane: golf outings, country clubs, private planes, and such. I associate with people who have made it financially, and I have to keep pace. But believe me, this kind of living is not what I see as my goal in life. I think I can prevent myself from being swallowed up by this lifestyle, but I have small children. They are going to grow up witnessing all of this. How do I convince them that this lifestyle is not the measure of happiness? Should I sell my business and home and move into a less affluent neighborhood?"

My counsel to Herbert was that there was no need to trade down for a less affluent environment *if* ... *if* he talked with his children about meaningful values; *if* the ambience in the home prevailed over the materialistic lifestyle; *if* he and his wife related with utmost consideration to each other; *if* they honored and respected their own parents; *if* they included the children in their charitable activities; *if* he showed restraint when provoked; *if* he could be humble in spite of his economic success—in other words, *if* he practiced the components of spirituality. The attitude in the home would foster spirituality in the children by example.

I once participated in a tribute event for a group of volunteers who donated several hours a week to spend time with shut-ins, driving them to the supermarket or doctor's office or playing a game with them. The theme of the evening was "Doing Good vs. Feeling Good." This theme stayed with me in my later work with drug addicts. I saw that addicts were totally absorbed with feeling good. They had no other interests or pursuits in life. I felt that if we could get people more involved in doing good, we might make progress in curtailing the drug-abuse epidemic.

One evening I met with a group of parents whose children were in treatment for drug abuse, and I conveyed to them my idea that, if they dedicated their families to "doing good" rather than just to "feeling good," they could exert an influence on their children that would lessen their likelihood of future drug use.

The following morning, the therapist said to me, "You made a strong point with the parents last night. After you left, I heard them say, 'Dr. Twerski is right! We have to get after our kids to do some volunteering.'"

Unfortunately, the parents had *not* heard my message. You don't "get after" your kids to do volunteering. You do it yourself, and then there is some chance that your children will emulate you. Establishing spirituality as the family's goal, and living spiritually, will encourage children to do likewise.

The Ultimate Goal

Most of our daily activities consist of many intermediate goals and purposes. We drive our cars to a gas station to get fuel, but if we have nowhere to go with the car, that purpose has little value. If we drive to work, we have a goal, but that, too, is an intermediate goal. Whatever we do at work is goal-directed, but these goals, too, may be intermediate goals. The bottom line is that intermediate goals cannot provide meaning in life.

Of course, we must have our physical and emotional needs satisfied, which requires many intermediate goals, but we must also be able to elevate ourselves above these. If we fail to do so, we can achieve only an animal quality of happiness, which is inadequate for humans.

Fulfillment for a caterpillar is to become a butterfly. Fulfillment for a tadpole is to become a frog. Fulfillment for a bear cub is to become an adult bear. Nature drives creatures to achieve their potential and to become the best they can be. Although the optimum goal for a caterpillar, tadpole, or bear cub is easily defined, the optimum for a human being is more complex and involves existential and philosophical concepts.

Bear with me while I go back to thinking about fish. Though fish in a tank cause me some discomfort, I have learned a valuable lesson from their distant cousins, the salmon. While visiting a salmon fishery on the West Coast, I witnessed the phenomenon of the salmon fighting the current, swimming uphill against the tide to return to their birthplace, spawn, and die. It was fascinating to watch the salmon leap over cascades. If they failed to make the leap, they would swim around a bit to restore their energy and try again to make the jump. They would persist in doing this until they succeeded.

The salmon probably does not think about why it is doing this. Its goal is instinctive, but it is determined to achieve it, and it does not allow obstacles to deter it. We humans do not have such a concrete, instinctive goal. Our ultimate goal is to *be the finest persons we can be*, and we need to use the full range of our intellectual and human abilities to achieve that goal.

I have said this many times, in many different forms, in this book, but here I want to insert an important word, for clarity: we have the ability to reflect on the purpose and goals of our lives. However, it is not necessarily *finding* a goal or a purpose that is fulfilling, but rather *contemplating and searching* for a goal and a purpose that makes us spiritual beings, happy beings.

There is an anecdote about two vagrants who were arrested for loitering and brought before a judge. The judge asked the first vagrant, "What were you doing when the officer arrested you?"

"Nothing," the vagrant answered.

The judge then turned to the second vagrant, "And what were you doing when you were arrested?"

The man pointed toward his buddy. "I was helping him," he said.

If we are helping someone who is doing nothing, we are doing nothing ourselves. That leaves us with an important question, "Where *do* we look for purpose?"

If the universe were not designed for a specific purpose but just happened to come about as a result of a freak accident that converted primordial energy into matter, which, over eons evolved into life on the planet Earth, then the world as a whole would have no specific purpose and there would be no ultimate purpose to human existence.

But if we believe that God created the world for a specific purpose and, via revelation or through prophets, instructed humans to live in a way that this purpose would be fulfilled, then we have an ultimate purpose. Because the concept of God involves attributes such as infinity, eternity, omniscience, and omnipresence—qualities with which humans have never had any sensory experience—it is a suprarational concept. All claims to prove the existence of God logically are subject to argument, and in the final analysis, belief in God requires a leap of faith. Indeed, natural disasters such as tsunamis, earthquakes, tornadoes, hurricanes, and incurable diseases defy any logical explanation of why a benevolent God would allow these to occur. A believer must go beyond logic to this leap of faith. People who have traversed this leap and have a firm conviction of God as the Creator of the universe can find a reason for an ultimate purpose in their existence.

You may have noted that I have not discussed religion as a *component* of spirituality. I do not want to confuse spirituality with religion; spirituality stands independent of religion. Although a person may be spiritual without being religious, the converse is not true. But I do think it is helpful to look at the *role* of religion.

If we wish to become better people, we must have some idea of what *good* is. Is wealth good? Is power good? Is knowledge good? Is acclaim good? If we seek to become wealthier, more powerful, more knowledgeable, or more famous, are we improving ourselves?

Spirituality requires trying to become a better person, but what defines better? An athlete may score more points due to the use of steroids. Is that a better athlete? A despotic ruler may increase his power through barbarism and betrayal. Is that a better ruler? A businesswoman may use devious means to make more money. Is greater wealth better? In order to preserve funds, one state (Oregon) will not cover certain medical procedures for people over eighty. Is this a good regulation?

Without religion, society is left to its own resources to establish a code of ethics and may operate on what is expedient rather than on what is morally correct. Religion can provide standards of right and wrong that are not altered by expedience. While it is true that people may distort religion for their own needs, religion can still provide guidelines that help us know how to be more considerate, more compassionate, more spiritual.

The relationship of spirituality to religion is depicted in this charming legend.

There were two brothers. One was childless, the other had a large family, and each had a farm. The childless brother thought, "My brother has many mouths to feed. I have only myself and my wife. I don't need that much." So, in the dark of the night, he would take a large bundle of grain and deposit it near his brother's house.

The other brother reckoned, "I am blessed with many children. My brother has no children. Perhaps his life could be just a bit sweeter if he had more bread." So, in the dark of the night, he would take a large bundle of grain and deposit it near his brother's house. Neither knew where the gifts of grain were coming from.

One night, the two brothers happened to meet, and they discovered the secret of the gifts. They embraced and cried on each other's shoulder. God looked down at the place where the two brothers met and chose it as the site for the Holy Temple.

That is the spirituality upon which all religion must be based. This is the spirituality of being the best we can be.

12

The Ability to
Search for Truth

Do animals misinterpret reality the way that people do? I think not. We humans are uniquely capable of distorting reality, often resulting in harmful consequences. We lie because we think it will be to our advantage. We misinterpret reality because we have a need to do so.

The psychiatrist Abraham Maslow made a simple but profound statement: "If all you have is a hammer, everything looks like a nail." We all have a need to feel useful. If I am an expert at fixing things, I am likely to see everything as broken. Our personal needs may cause us to misinterpret reality and to distort truth.

Yet as much as we have the ability to distort truth, we surely have the unique ability to search for truth. This quest, however, is replete with pitfalls. The human intellect is extremely vulnerable to distortion by the human will. Rationalization is one of the mind's shrewdest maneuvers, and the ability of our minds to defend our desires is truly remarkable.

Rationalization vs. Truth

A customer in a camera store bargained with the proprietor for a lower price. Reluctantly, the proprietor lowered the price, and the man bought the camera and paid in cash. After the man left the store, the proprietor counted the money and found that the man had erroneously paid fifty dollars more than the agreed-upon price. The proprietor could have called the man back and returned the excess money, but instead she reasoned, "This is really the money he should have paid." She did not feel she was doing wrong by keeping the excess money, even though she had agreed to the lesser amount.

Rationalization is an interesting phenomenon. We use it most often not to justify our behavior to *others*, but to convince *ourselves* of what we wish to believe. We find *logical* reasons to defend our behavior instead of *true* reasons. And though we end up deceiving ourselves, we may feel very satisfied with how we got there.

A very logical rationalization fueled by an intense emotional drive may have formidable tenacity. Any argument that challenges the conclusion of such a rationalization is likely to be rebutted or simply ignored. A recovering alcoholic once said, "In my thirty years of drinking, I never took a drink unless I had concluded that it was the right thing to do at that point."

This is the way desires for self-gratification subvert the quest for truth. A sincere search for the truth requires that we try to find reasons for concepts that are *contrary* to our beliefs. Researchers, for example, have been known to overlook findings that tend to disprove their theories, not because they are dishonest, but because their desire to prove their theory blinds them to any facts that may disprove it. Researchers who are sincere in their quest for truth will list the various hypotheses that disagree with their theory.

Lawyers may use a similar technique to convince jurors of the truth. A highly successful attorney once told me, "I know that the jury thinks I can see only those things that favor my client. When I present my case, I first list all the arguments in favor of the *other* litigant, and I show the jury in what way these arguments have merit. *Then* I go on to dismantle all these points. That way the jury knows that I have given serious consideration to the opponent's viewpoint, and they will be more inclined to believe my client."

Perhaps you have had this common experience: when your alarm clock rings, you dream a scene in which there is the ringing of a bell. This is your mind's way of allowing you to sleep longer and ignore the alarm clock. But just think: your mind could not have fabricated that scene until the alarm clock rang. Within a fraction of a second, your mind conjured up a complex scene to protect your sleep! Similarly, our minds can ingeniously conjure up a variety of reasons to justify gratifying a desire, and we may believe these reasons because we *want* to.

The "quest for truth" component of spirituality, therefore, requires that we be alert to our all-too-human "quest for justification."

Honesty vs. Truth

Since human motivation most often has its source in emotion rather than in intellect, how can we avoid the pitfall of self-deception?

This question was posed to a theologian, who gave the following answer: "A tightrope walker maintains his delicate balance in the following manner. When he feels himself being pulled to one side, he overcorrects by leaning a bit to the opposite side. If he corrected only to the center, he would fall.

"If you feel motivated to do something, realize that most motivation originates in desire. Therefore, think of reasons why you should *not* do it. This overcorrection may help counteract the rationalizations."

When we are attacked, our instinctive response is to defend ourselves. This is equally true when the attack is against our opinions and beliefs as when it is against our person: we want to be right. Our minds can immediately conjure up any number of arguments to defend our position, and the urge to be right may reinforce our convictions. This is good reason why, in order to avoid self-deception, we need to seek the opinions of those who can be more objective than we are because they are not subject to the same drives that motivate us.

Many of the philosophers of yore, such as Diogenes with his lantern, sought truth, but the post-modern world is often motivated by expedience rather than by a quest for truth. In his book *Why Religion Matters,* Huston Smith points out that early in Harvard's history, one of its presidents cited the statement of Aristotle, "Find a friend in Plato, a friend in Socrates, but above all, find a friend in Truth." Smith goes on to cite Wilfred Cantwell Smith's statement that although *veritas* remains enshrined on the insignia of Harvard University, the word does not once appear in a statement on the aims of undergraduate education that its faculty took two years to hammer out.

Truth is more than an abstract concept. It involves putting the best we can be into action. There was a woman who bought a covered frying pan, and she placed the cover on the pan as she laid it on the checkout counter. But there were actually two price tags: the pan was $9.98 and the cover was $2.98. The clerk, seeing only the price tag on the cover, assumed that the entire item was $2.98 and rang it up as such. The woman said to her, "That's not right. The $2.98 is only for the cover. The pan is $9.98."

This woman could have saved ten dollars by remaining silent. However, she was truthful.

The bottom line is that honesty and truth are inseparable. A spiritual person who sincerely searches for truth must be prepared to accept the consequences of truth whatever they may be, even if the truth is uncomfortable. The temporary unhappiness of discomfort may well be, in the end, the only way to true happiness.

Seeking vs. Finding Truth

Relief from Spiritual Deficiency Syndrome does not require *finding* truth. It is not *arriving* at the truth but rather *searching* for the truth with sincerity, unaffected by ulterior motives, that makes a person spiritual. Truthfulness is more than a noble trait. Some people have made a fortune by lying and deception, but lasting success—and lasting happiness—can come only with truth.

One of my patients in the psychiatric hospital had many physical complaints that I felt were "drug-seeking." I told the nurse to give the patient an injection of saline. He would feel the stick and the smart of the saline and believe he had received medication. I was surprised when the nurse told me that the medical director forbade the use of placebos.

Curious, I asked the medical director for an explanation. As a general medicine intern, I had often prescribed placebos. The medical director replied, "Dr. Twerski, before we came out of the trees and developed speech, we communicated like all other animals—nonverbally. When we developed verbal communication, we did not eliminate nonverbal communication, but rather superimposed speech on it. We, therefore, communicate in both ways, verbally and nonverbally.

"While we do have control of what we say, we have little or no control over our nonverbal communications. If you give a patient a placebo, you are saying verbally, 'I am giving you something,' but your nonverbal communication is saying, 'I am giving you nothing.' Your patient receives both messages, is confused, and his trust in you is impaired.

"Your single most important tool in psychiatry is the patient's trust. You can't afford to jeopardize it."

Realizing the truth in that, I stopped lying. I realized that I could not be a good liar. (Trust me, neither can you.) I needed to believe in what I was doing, not offer placebos.

There's a story that illustrates the need to believe in something yourself in order to successfully communicate it to others. Mark Twain said, "You can't *pray* a lie" [italics mine]. Similarly, I believe that we cannot *communicate* a lie. A lie is always a double message because our nonverbal messages get communicated along with our spoken messages. Verbal messages are from the conscious mind of the speaker to the conscious mind of the listener. Nonverbal communication is from one unconscious mind to another unconscious mind. At the unconscious level, listeners know when they are being lied to.

During World War II, a family of my father's congregation received a message that their soldier son was missing in action in the European theater of war. Understandably, the parents were crushed by this news. My father tried to comfort them by saying that missing in action did not mean that he had been killed, that very likely he was a prisoner of war and would return when the war was over.

Once a week, my father visited their home to comfort them and to keep up their hopes that their son was alive. Indeed, after V-E Day, the parents received the glad tidings that their son had been a prisoner of war and had been liberated.

When the son returned to his base, he found a pile of letters from my father. For two years, my father had written him a letter every week.

What was the point of writing those letters? My father wrote them each week before he went to visit the parents. In order to help the parents keep up their hopes that their son was alive, my father had to reinforce this belief in himself. If he had not believed it, his words to the parents would have had little effect because the nonverbal message would have betrayed his true feelings.

Throughout the pages of this book, I have been focusing on the superiority of humans over animals. But in this arena, I sometimes wonder if, at least in one way, animals may be superior to us. *Animals cannot lie!* They are truthful creatures.

What is the truth? When does a "kind" misstatement become a lie? When does a "justified" action become a problem? Can honesty ever be a "bad" thing? Each of us will wrestle with these kinds of questions all of our days, but the point of reassurance comes not when we find the one truth, but when we know we are continually on the path of seeking the truths that reflect our beliefs, our purpose, and our God. That is when we will be able to lay a claim to our corner of happiness.

13

The Ability to
Change

Iwas in my second year of psychiatric training when I received a call
from the psych emergency room. A woman said she had to see a psychiatrist promptly and could not wait for an appointment. Psych emer-
gencies are usually suicide threats or some other acute crisis, so I took her
seriously. There was not, however, an emergency. To this day I'm not sure
why Isabel came to the emergency room, but I'm glad she did. The story
she told me was an unusual one: she had asked to be placed in a state mental institution for a year! Isabel's visit changed the entire course of my life.

She was one of three daughters of an Episcopalian priest. Late in
adolescence, she had started drinking, and by age twenty, she was into
very heavy drinking. She married and had a child, but by the time the
child turned three, her husband gave her an ultimatum: "Make your
choice. It's either the booze or the family."

"I knew I could not stop drinking," Isabel said, "and I wasn't
much of a wife or mother. It was only decent to give him the divorce
he asked for."

I could see that even now at sixty-one, Isabel was attractive, so she
must have been stunning at twenty-eight. Free and unattached, she began
serving as an escort to some of Pittsburgh's social elite. She had a beautiful apartment, the latest in fashions, and all the alcohol she wanted.

After five years, the alcohol began to cause behavioral changes. She started serving a lower socioeconomic clientele and very rapidly deteriorated. She was soon living in fleabag hotels and prostituting.

Every so often, someone found her passed out and took her to a hospital for detoxification. She would attend the AA meetings in the hospital, but upon discharge, would promptly resume drinking. Between 1938 and 1956, Isabel had been detoxified at St. Francis Hospital fifty-nine times! That didn't even count the other twenty-two admissions at another hospital. Her family had, and would, hang up if she called them.

In 1956, Isabel approached a lawyer who had helped her out of some alcohol-related jams. "David, I need a favor," she said.

"Good God!" the lawyer said. "Not again! What did you do this time?"

"I'm not in any trouble," Isabel said. "I want you to put me away in the state hospital for a year."

At that time Pennsylvania statutes had an Inebriate Act, under which a chronic alcoholic could be committed to a state hospital for "a year and one day." This law had been used by families who wanted to get a chronic alcoholic out of their hair, but no alcoholic had ever *asked* to be put away in a state mental hospital for a year.

"You don't know what you're asking for," the lawyer said. "You're crazy."

"If I'm crazy, I really belong in the state hospital," Isabel replied.

Isabel continued to press her request, and the lawyer finally took her before the judge and had her committed to the state hospital.

After a year of sobriety, Isabel left the state hospital and promptly went to an AA meeting. Someone gave her a few nights of shelter, and she soon found a job as a housekeeper for a nationally renowned physician.

I had never heard anything like this before. My seminary training as a rabbi had taught me nothing about alcoholism. Medical school was no better. I learned a lot about some rare diseases but nothing about addictions, which may well be the most common disease a doctor encounters. As a fledgling psychiatrist, I knew that there had to be motivation for a person to seek help. What could possibly have motivated Isabel to take so drastic a measure as to put herself into a state mental hospital for a year by a court order?

In the next session I heard some more interesting stories. I was curious how she was managing to stay sober. It was obvious to me that medicine and psychiatry at that time had no effective treatment for alcoholism. What was her secret?

"I go to meetings of Alcoholics Anonymous," she said.

You have to remember that this was back in 1961, and celebrities had not yet revealed that they were recovering alcoholics. Few people outside of AA even knew anything about it.

"What happens at these meetings?" I asked. "Who provides the treatment?"

"We have speaker's meetings and discussion meetings, and we share our experiences," Isabel said.

"Do you have psychiatrists or psychologists there?" I asked.

Isabel said, "There is one psychologist who shows up occasionally, but he's still drunk most of the time."

"Look, Isabel," I said. "Some kind of treatment must be going on at these meetings, if they are keeping you sober. Can I come and see for myself?"

"Sure," Isabel said. That week she took me to my first AA meeting.

The first thing that struck me at the meeting was that there was no stratification. What impressed me about AA was that once people entered the room, everyone was equal. The rich received no special attention. Sometimes a poor person was in the position to help a wealthy person. Nor did academic status count. A fifth-grade dropout and a PhD were treated equally. I had never encountered anything like this!

I never did solve that mystery of why Isabel chose to put herself into a state hospital, but I have some ideas. Likewise, I never determined what, exactly, brought Isabel to the emergency room that day.

My personal belief is that she was sent to change the course of my life. Her sender? Your guess is as good as mine.

Do you know how a volcano is formed? Deep down at the core of the Earth, there is melted rock that is under extreme pressure. Over many centuries, this lava slowly makes its way through fissures in the Earth's crust to the surface. Once it breaks through the surface, the lava erupts.

At the core of every human being, I believe there is a nucleus of self-respect and dignity, a desire for self-fulfillment, that will always break through. For a variety of reasons, this nucleus may be concealed and suppressed. Like the lava, it seeks to break through the surface and be recognized. Once it erupts into our awareness, we may feel, "I am too good to be acting this way. This behavior is beneath my dignity." I think this is the spiritual awakening to which the twelfth step of the AA program refers.

I also think that this is what happened to Isabel. For years she had been blind to her self-worth and had seen nothing wrong with her alcoholic behavior. She was motivated by nothing other than self-gratification. Then one day, the nucleus of self-respect that had been buried deep within her broke through the surface, and she realized that she no longer wanted to demean herself. She was a human being who could be spiritual, not an animal that could not be anything other than self-centered. She faced her Spiritual Deficiency Syndrome with incredible courage.

It Is Never Too Late

I do most of my writing early in the morning, when my mind is rested. One time a publisher told me they were moving the publishing date and I would have to complete the book sooner. That meant that I had to get up an hour earlier.

I set my alarm clock for 4:30 a.m. When it rang, I did what most people would do: I turned it off for just five minutes more of sleep. Of course, I woke up two hours later.

Several months after that, I had to deliver a lecture in Washington, D.C., at 10 a.m., which required taking a 7 a.m. flight. To make this flight, I had to be up at 5 a.m. Knowing my tendency to turn off the alarm for "just five more minutes," I took precautions so that I would not miss my flight. I took the alarm clock off the nightstand and set it in the far corner of the room so that I could not turn it off from the bed. The next morning I awoke at 5 a.m. and had to walk across the room to turn off the alarm. I was then able to stay awake and make the flight.

On both occasions, I had an "awakening." The first awakening did not last long because I went back to sleep. The second time I did something to avoid going right back to sleep; I made the awakening last.

Some people may have a spiritual awakening, but it does not last. Isabel knew that unless she took some measure to make her awakening last, she was likely to revert to drinking. The only way she knew to keep her awakening alive was to put herself out of reach of alcohol for an extended period of time. She saw the state hospital as her only option.

Many people are so preoccupied with work, and feel the pressure for tending to so many things in our complex civilization, that they may not have the time or leisure to give serious thought to self-fulfillment or spirituality. Their first opportunity may not come until retirement, but then some may think, "It's too late to make any major changes in my lifestyle."

It is never too late. Although the greater part of Isabel's adult life was spent in dissolute behavior, in the last seventeen years of her life, she more than redeemed herself. Isabel became a spiritual person, and in working toward self-fulfillment, she helped many people overcome the scourge of alcoholism.

To be happy, each of us must have faith in ourselves and be willing to put forth the effort to maximize our potential. The story below exemplifies this willingness to work toward becoming the best a person can be.

Henry's mother was advised to put Henry in a special school because he was unable to understand what other children grasped easily. Henry cried himself to sleep. His mother took Henry and consulted her pastor, who said, "How can they say that Henry is dumb? Why, he's smarter than most of the other kids!"

"That's all I needed to hear," Henry told me. "I just had to work harder to activate my brain." Henry went on to become a highly successful attorney, graduating from law school with honors.

Just as our bodies need proper nutrition and judicious exercise, so too do our spirits need spiritual nutrients. Happiness is a healthy human spirit well nourished by being the best we have the capability of being.

Part 3

10 STEPS
to HAPPINESS

The natural state of all matter is *inertia*. Objects stay at rest until something moves them. Living things, too, stay at rest until something causes them to move (motivation). Movement of any stationary object requires exerting force, and anything that requires effort is likely to meet with resistance.

That explains a lot about why it is so hard for us to change. Deciding to be a better person, a more spiritual person, a happier person—as good as all that sounds—is not the easiest thing to do. We, too, are likely to meet with resistance—our own! We, too, will have to put forth some effort.

Sitting in a dentist's waiting room, I came across an article titled "How Do Lobsters Grow?" Come to think of it, how *can* a lobster grow? It is encased in an inflexible shell that does not expand.

The answer is that the lobster grows until the shell becomes confining and oppressive. The lobster then retreats under a rock to be safe from predatory fish, sheds the shell, and produces a more spacious one. As the lobster continues to grow, the new shell will also eventually become oppressive, and the lobster will repeat the process of shedding the confining shell and producing a larger shell.

The signal for the lobster that it is time to shed its shell, so that it can continue to grow, is *discomfort*! Just think: if lobsters had access to doctors, they might never grow. Every time they felt the discomfort of the oppressive shell, they would get a prescription for a painkiller or a tranquilizer. With the discomfort gone, they would not shed the shell and produce a more spacious one. They would die as tiny little lobsters.

The same is true for human beings: discomfort is often a signal that it is time to grow. One reason people may fail to grow spiritually is that they ignore, or try to mask, the signals. We are all too ready to reach for medications or pleasures or extra activity to relieve our discomfort.

At one AA meeting, a speaker was relating the misery he had experienced during his active addiction. Then he challenged the audience with this question: "Can anyone tell me anything they have ever learned from a pleasurable experience?"

I had never thought of it quite that way. I could not think of anything I had *learned* from a really enjoyable experience (other than wanting to repeat it).

To grow spiritually requires that we do two things: reinforce our positive character traits and reduce our negative character traits. This takes self-awareness and learning. We need to *know* what our strengths and shortcomings are before we can decide how we want to use or change them. One person stated this in a rather picturesque manner: "Man is half angel and half s.o.b., and that's okay."

Understandably, we may resist acknowledging negative traits, but if we recognize that the human makeup is body plus spirit, *and* that the body is essentially an animal body with all the drives and impulses that animals have, we can accept that we are "half s.o.b."

While we may recognize the need for self-awareness, actually doing a self-assessment may be uncomfortable, especially when it comes to admitting where we fall short. It's hard to face our faults. Many of us don't want to believe that we are capable of harboring feelings we consider odious. So it's not surprising that it is hard to acknowledge our negative traits. Some may find it even harder to acknowledge their positive traits. They may be reluctant to identify their assets because this awareness implies a responsibility to activate and maximize these potentials. Some would rather coast along than put forth the effort. But if we can hold on to the thought that discomfort is a sign of growth, the discomfort of self-assessment will be more than offset by the greater reward of healthy self-awareness. The following story illustrates my point.

A young woman was in an automobile accident and sustained several serious injuries. The fracture of her right shoulder had severed several of the nerves from the spinal cord to the right arm, and she had lost all motion and sensation in her right arm. The surgeons had done a nerve repair, reconnecting the torn nerves. However, nerves are not like an electric wire. Connecting the two ends of the nerve does not restore its function. The nerve will function only if the fibers from the proximal segment grow down into the distal segment. The doctors had told her that it would be several months before they could determine whether the nerve function was restored. They placed her arm in a sling, and she had to wait patiently, not knowing whether she would ever regain the use of her right arm.

One day a few months later, she was playing cards with friends and smoking a cigarette, which she held in her left hand together with the cards. As she tried to move the cards, the cigarette fell onto her right hand, and she felt the burn. She promptly threw her cards into the air and jumped ecstatically, joyously shouting, "I'm hurting! I'm hurting!"

Feeling pain is not usually a cause for joy. However, for this woman, the pain was an indication that the nerves had grown properly and that she would regain the function of her right arm. Compared to that joy, the pain of the burn was insignificant.

"Okay," you may be saying, "I understand that if I want to be happier, I need to be willing to face the potential discomfort of self-awareness. I'm ready. I would like to be the best person I can be, but just how do I go about achieving that?"

If you can make this statement, it means you're *already* on the path because you are *already aware* that you are not yet the best you can be. If you feel you've achieved your full potential and have become the ideal human being, there's no need to read further! But if you're ready to grow beyond where you are, this final section of the book offers a process of ten steps that will bring more happiness into your life. There are no deadlines for this process, no tests, no grades, no judges.

In the human species, physical growth stops in late adolescence/ early adulthood. In fact, our bodies reach their zenith at this point and start down the road to deterioration! But spiritual growth can continue as long as we have a functioning mind. The work of spirituality, becoming the best we can be, is essentially a *transformation*. It begins with one step, then another, and another. You need only respond to the invitation to grow. There is no end point, only continuing gifts of discovery along the way—and the potential to find a truer happiness than you've ever known.

Step 1

*"I am aware that I have some shortcomings,
and I want to become a better person."*

Since becoming a better person requires time and effort, you will make this investment only if *becoming the best person you can be* is sufficiently important to you.

Now, my handwriting is far from the best, and there is no question that if I put more time and effort into improving my penmanship, I could do so. But I don't do that because having beautiful handwriting is just not that important to me. Violin and piano virtuosos, on the other hand, who are the acknowledged masters in their fields, practice hours every day because being the best musicians they can be is of utmost importance to them.

If you have decided that *becoming the best person you can be* is important to you, it's going to take practice. You'll need to do some things to make it happen. Here's an example.

A young salesman approached a farmer and began to talk excitedly about the book he was carrying. "This book will tell you everything you need to know about farming," he said. "It tells you when to sow and when to reap. It tells you about the weather, what to expect, and when to expect it. This book tells you all you need to know."

"Young man," the farmer said, "that's not the problem. I know everything that is in that book. My problem is doing it."

If you have read this far, you have read a great deal about what it takes to be a spiritual person. The problem is doing it.

The first step begins with *keeping a journal.* I'm going to ask you to jump right in with perhaps the hardest task of all: recognizing that you have shortcomings. I want you to write a list in your journal of all the shortcomings you can think of. Don't let your internal censors kick in. This journal is private, for your eyes only. Being honest with yourself is the only place to begin. (But I will add this word of caution: what you think of as your shortcomings may not be the way others see them. You might have a tendency to be very critical of yourself, and you may see "defects" that are not really there, or they may not be as bad as you make them out to be. At some point in the process of these ten steps, you might want to check this out with people whom you trust.)

Your journal entries may look something like this:

I am impatient. I want things to happen right away.
I have a short fuse and can explode in anger.
I procrastinate.
I'm very sensitive and am easily offended.
I can be very stubborn.
I have many fears.
I don't trust people.
I can't stand my partner's family.

Once you have made your initial list (remember: you can always add to it or change it), it is helpful to clarify the picture by giving examples from real-life situations. For example:

I am impatient. If the driver in front of me is going too slow and I can't pass him, I keep blinking my headlights. I hit the horn repeatedly and curse under my breath. Just because he has all day doesn't mean that I have.

I have a short fuse and can explode in anger. I told my wife to pick me up at 3 p.m. to drive me to the airport. I like to allow plenty of time, so if we encounter a traffic jam, I won't be late for the flight. But my wife didn't come until 3:15, and I screamed at her.

Write your incidents in your journal as soon as possible after they happen. That will give you the opportunity to review them later when you are *not* upset.

Now you are ready to move on to step 2.

Step 2

*"I realize that I can be in charge
of my behavior."*

The advantage of writing your shortcomings in a journal is that it gives you a chance to review your responses when you are not in the middle of experiencing them. Go back for a moment to the example in step 1 about the slow driver. If you're in a situation like this where you get agitated, you may not be able to think clearly at the time. But when you're away from the situation and not under pressure, you can reconsider it in a different light.

Do you know the Serenity Prayer?

> God, grant me the serenity to accept the things I cannot change,
> the courage to change the things I can, and the wisdom to know
> the difference.

This is a very practical way to live. If something can't be changed, then you really have no other choice but to accept the reality. Accepting it does not mean you *approve* of it (just as you don't "approve" of a tsunami or a hurricane), but denying that it happened is foolish, so you need to accept the reality.

The reality is, if one slow driver did not respond to your blinking or horn-tooting, another slow driver is not likely to do anything different the next time it happens—and it *will* happen again. Cursing under your breath is not going to make someone go faster, so you're wasting your energy and working yourself into a frenzy that can stress your heart and give you a migraine headache. Sure, it's irritating, but there's no point in taking it out on your body.

While you cannot control another person's behavior, you can be in control of your own. When you take the time to reflect on your actions, you have a chance to think about what you might do differently the next time the driver ahead of you doesn't respond. Here's where the serenity comes in. You're stuck behind a slow car—that's a fact, and the situation is not changing. To avoid punishing your body, instead of cursing under your breath, you could sing or whistle or hum a tune. I keep a tape of calming music in the car, and when I am stuck in a traffic jam or behind a slow driver, I listen to the music. It is amazing how that reduces my irritation.

Here's another example. Imagine that you're the one who wrote in step 1 about being upset at the late arrival of your wife (or husband). As you reflect on the situation, you realize that screaming did not result in getting to the airport any earlier, which is what you really wanted. If screaming is not going to help, why scream?

But that's not the first time your spouse has been late. I understand. It's truly annoying. But do you really think that screaming will make someone arrive on time? When you scream at people, they tune you out. Your message won't come through. Besides, they may get defensive and scream back, "It's not my fault there was a disabled vehicle blocking traffic! Can't you understand that such things happen? Haven't you ever been caught in a traffic jam?"

So you decide not to scream. Instead, when you return from the trip, you might say, "Honey, I did make the flight on time. But I like to leave extra time just in case there is heavy traffic. You don't want me to miss the flight any more than I do. I suppose I *could* have told you that I needed to be picked up at 2:45, to make *sure* that you would be there by 3:00, but I don't want to play that game with you. Please leave the house early enough, just in case we encounter traffic." That is much more likely to get the results you want than screaming is.

Now it's your turn. Take some time to review the reactions you wrote in your journal in step 1. Give some thought to how you might respond differently the next time. Then, when you try out a new behavior, record the details of this experience in your journal the first chance you get. Describe how you handled the situation differently and include how you felt.

There may be times when you will record a loss of control and other times when you will see how you were able to "take the higher ground." I want to add one more word here about this idea of "self-control." Don't confuse controlling yourself with controlling others; they are polar opposites. If you seek to control others, you will evoke resentment and preclude being loved. If you control yourself by restraining your anger and letting go of grudges, you are lovable.

An interesting thing will happen as you review your log over a period of time: you will begin to see what responses are the most effective. Pay particular attention to the new behaviors that you would describe as "your human spirit at its best." These are the changes that will bring you the most happiness.

Step 3

"I realize that changing my character traits is a slow process, but I am willing to persist. I'm going to work on my character defects, one by one."

This is an important step.

Most of your character traits have been with you for a long time, even as early as childhood. A long-standing trait cannot be changed radically overnight. In fact, I would say it is probably easier to get a PhD than to change even a single character trait. Your process of change will be gradual, and it is normal to have relapses along the way. And if you try to do too much at one time, you may accomplish nothing. Alcoholics Anonymous recognized that, for the alcoholic, the thought that "I can never drink again" appears to be an impossibility. The alcoholic would see no reason to even try if failure were a foregone conclusion. AA, therefore, advocates taking "one day at a time." That is bite-size progress and can be realistically handled. Similarly, trying to transform your personality all at once is likely to fail. You will be much more successful—and happier—if you concentrate on improving one trait at a time.

So, the question is, where to start?

But first, a few words about how feelings can be modified.

It is probable that actions have a greater impact on feelings than feelings have on actions. In other words, the way you act influences the way you feel. Charles Schulz illustrates this point in the following *Peanuts* cartoon strip about Sally:

Just as Sally's "inner peace" did nothing to alter her obnoxious behavior, so, too, your "inner peace" may not be reflected in your behavior quite the way you wanted. However, behaving courteously and empathetically may result in the development of inner peace. To put it another way, ideas may not change behavior, but *behavior may change ideas*. For example, if you are carrying a grudge against someone and you want to change this, you can lessen and eventually eliminate the grudge by *doing something nice for that person*. Look for an opportunity where you can do this person a kindness. The more you do this, the lesser your grudge will be.

You might be thinking, "The last thing I want to do is be nice to that person." Remember, you are not doing this for *someone else*. You are doing this to improve *your* character, to be more spiritual, to be a happier person.

Improving yourself one defect at a time may have a wide impact. Take this example: a woman decided to replace a shabby, worn-out living room chair. The new chair clashed with the old sofa, so the sofa had to be replaced. But then the carpet was out of place. Eventually, the carpet, wallpaper, lamps, and pictures had to be replaced. The entire living room underwent a change as a result of a single new chair.

This is true of character traits as well. Improving one trait may result in other traits being incompatible and may result in a total character overhaul.

So, where do you want to start? What character trait bugs you the most? (Or, perhaps, bugs other people the most?) It is important to choose only *one* shortcoming for step 3. Record a statement in your journal that reads something like the samples below, filling in the blanks as you go.

I have decided to work on this character defect:

It causes problems when:

I am prepared for other things to start changing as well!
  I am ready to be a better, happier person by working on this
  (insert trait):

Step 4

"I am going to look for ways to overcome my negative character traits."

Once you have identified the character trait you want to improve, the next step is to look for ways you might begin to do this. By writing down the trait you want to change, you've already taken a step toward overcoming this negative in your life: you've recognized that it exists! There are many options available to you, from consulting competent people who can help you, to reading books on character improvement (see the Suggestions for Further Reading section at the back of this book for some ideas).

Life stories of spiritual people, such as the biographies of Gandhi, Mother Teresa, Albert Schweitzer, and other spiritual people are excellent sources for spiritual development. These people were human beings, like all of us, who exemplified fulfillment of the unique traits that comprise spirituality. No one is expecting you to reach the lofty heights of these extraordinary people, just as an amateur violinist does not necessarily become an Itzhak Perlman, a world-renowned violinist known for his unmistakable musicianship and love of music. Yet, an amateur violinist will make every effort to attend an Itzhak Perlman performance because it will inspire him or her to achieve greater excellence. Similarly, the stories of people who reach extraordinary spiritual heights will inspire you to exert greater efforts to become more spiritual.

Although it is beyond the scope of this book to provide guidelines for overcoming all the negative traits we humans possess, I'll point out a few ways, to "jump-start" your thinking:

CHANGING DISAPPROVAL TO EMPATHY

An excellent way to develop empathy is to live by the Golden Rule: "Do unto others as you would have others do unto you."

As we know, the human mind is ingenious at rationalizing, conjuring up all kinds of reasons to justify something we have done or want to do. See what happens when you apply this ability to others. When you see someone doing something of which you disapprove—even if it is something directed at you—try rationalizing why this person may be doing it.

If someone's action offends you, consider this: perhaps he's had a bad day. Maybe she just had a tax audit. Maybe his wife walked out on him. Maybe she lost her job. These are ways of recognizing the stress other people may be under and, as the saying goes, "feeling their pain." Try justifying *other people's* behavior as you might justify your own.

CHANGING INTOLERANCE TO TOLERANCE

The first thing you can practice to overcome intolerance is to accept your own limitations. If you can accept that *everyone* has limitations—and that you are not better or different from anyone else when it comes to human flaws—this commonality, or as Ernst Kurtz terms it in *The Spirituality of Imperfection*, our "shared weakness"—will go a long way toward helping you be tolerant of others.

Kurtz suggests that, just as a violinist develops skillful playing by beginning with simple, easy pieces, then moving on to more difficult pieces, so, too, can you develop tolerance by first practicing it on people you love and respect, then extending it to people whom you don't like.

It might be helpful to put yourself in situations where you have more opportunities to practice tolerance. If you always surround yourself with people who are of like thinking, you are at a disadvantage when you need to interact with people who differ from you.

CHANGING SELF-DECEIT TO THE QUEST FOR TRUTH

Truth can be very elusive because the clever mental mechanisms you are endowed with may lead you to believe what you *want* to believe is true. Self-interest can distort your judgment, sometimes in ways so subtle you may not even recognize it, even during a careful soul searching. You may need an objective observer to set you straight—I know, I've been there.

When I was in my fourth year of medical school, I received a call from a hospital that a woman wished to see a rabbi. It was almost midnight when I arrived at the hospital, and I was directed to the neonatal intensive care unit, where a woman was standing next to an incubator. She told me that her newborn baby had a congenital heart defect that was not correctable surgically, and that the baby was going to die. She looked at me tearfully and said, "Why, Rabbi, why?"

Of course, I had no answer for her. I stayed with her, sharing the silence. Then I said, "Do you feel like praying?" When she said that she did, I said a brief prayer with her.

The next morning, I told my father about this and said that I could not help feeling angry at God. What was the purpose of this woman going through nine months of pregnancy, dreaming of the joy a child would bring her, only to be dealt so crushing a blow, to have to watch her baby die? Why does God allow so much agony for a futility?

My father said that we cannot understand many things that God does, and that we must have faith that, in the divine plan, everything has a place. "This woman is not the same woman she was. This painful experience has made a change in her. Although we cannot understand it, it was not futile."

Then my father continued: "Are you sure that your anger at God is because of this woman's pain? Might it be because of your own?"

"I don't understand," I said.

"You are a rabbi," he said, "and now you have added also being a doctor. You embody the two most powerful helping and healing professions, yet you felt you were unable to do anything for this woman. Was it perhaps your feeling of impotence that made you angry? Were you feeling more sorry for yourself than for the woman?"

I didn't want to think that might be true. I didn't want to think that I was so selfish, that instead of feeling the woman's pain, I was nursing an ego wound.

But I could not escape the truth. My father was right. I was deceiving myself that I was concerned only for this woman.

I returned to the hospital a number of times, and I was there when the woman's baby died. When she thanked me, I realized that I had not been totally impotent after all. I had given of myself and kept her from being alone in her distress.

I had thought I was feeling sorry for the woman, but in reality I was feeling sorry for myself. I could not have discovered this by myself. It took an outside observer to set me straight.

CHANGING VANITY TO HUMILITY

What was my ego pain all about? I had not accepted my reality as a human being with many limitations. I lacked the humility of accepting myself. I wanted to be not only 100 percent angel, but I also wanted to be all-powerful. My grandiosity made me feel inadequate when I was not only unable to save the infant's life as a doctor, but also, as a rabbi, not able to give the woman an explanation of why this was happening. My vanity would not allow me to accept my powerlessness.

To be humble, you need to accept reality. That does not mean you need to put yourself down! Humility does not mean self-abasement. If you are gifted in some areas, recognize your strengths. But it also means not considering yourself to be better than other people. Dag Hammarskjöld put it well in his classic book *Markings*: "To be humble is not to make comparisons." Relate to everyone respectfully, and you will be on your way toward humility.

CHANGING RESENTMENT TO FORGIVENESS

Although you have no choice whether or not to feel anger when provoked, you do have some control over how long you will continue to feel angry. If you hang on to your anger, it will turn into a grudge or a resentment, and harboring resentments is toxic and self-defeating. Holding on to anger is particularly toxic within the family and it can lead to abuse and ruin a marriage. Children may cower before you if they fear your anger. They may abide by what you say, but they cannot really love you. Love and fear are mutually exclusive.

Letting go of resentments is *forgiving*, which is a uniquely human and spiritual trait. However, it is not easy to forgive someone who has hurt you. You might be thinking, "I will never forgive him for what he did to me," or "I can't forget how she misled me." I understand that, but how is that going to improve the situation or make you feel better? What is there to gain by *not* forgiving?

Forgiving others is not only healthy from a physiological standpoint, but it also has an important psychological benefit because when you practice forgiveness of *others*, you understand that *you, too, can be forgiven*. If you do not feel you can be forgiven, you will not be able to rid yourself of guilt.

A recovering alcoholic helped me realize the toxicity of harboring a grudge. This man had been exploited and dealt with grossly unfairly. He said, "I am full of anger and bitterness at those people, but I will go to an AA meeting today and try to divest myself of these resentments, because if I hang on to resentments, I will drink again."

It occurred to me that this man was fortunate in being aware that harboring resentments is destructive. Most people who bear grudges are not aware that these may cause migraine headaches, high blood pressure, or other psychosomatic conditions.

I was curious just how Alcoholics Anonymous could help him eliminate his resentments, so I accompanied him to a meeting. When he shared his feelings, a veteran in recovery said, "Hanging on to resentments is allowing someone you dislike to live inside your head without paying rent. Why would you be so foolish? The person whom you dislike doesn't care how you feel about him. You are the one who is tormented by resentments. Why punish yourself for another person's misbehavior?"

This is a powerful question to take to heart.

While animals lack the ability to rid themselves of resentments—they'll attack their assailant at the first opportunity—you have a choice. Deciding how you will react to provocation and seeking to divest yourself of resentment is a step toward self-fulfillment and spirituality.

My father taught me a good way to let go of resentment. If someone offended him, he would say, "If that person would have realized that his action was wrong, he would not have done it. I feel sorry for him that he was so ignorant. Pity and anger cannot coexist. I can't be angry at him when I feel sorry for him."

CHANGING COMPLACENCE TO GRATITUDE

Gratitude is not innate. Animals do not naturally demonstrate gratitude. True, domesticated pets seem to be able to express gratitude, but that is because they have absorbed this ability from their close association with humans. Animals in the wild do not express gratitude because it is a human, spiritual trait that needs to be developed.

Children sometimes have difficulty in expressing gratitude. It is not unusual for a mother to tell her five-year-old child, "Say 'thank you' to the nice person for the candy," and get only a grunt as a response.

Adults may have difficulty not only in expressing gratitude, but also even *feeling* gratitude. This may be because when someone does us a kindness, we may feel obligated to that person, and in order to avoid feeling obligated, our minds do a defensive maneuver and make us deny that we have been the recipient of kindness. Or it may be because we don't fully appreciate what we have. Whatever the reasons, it is worth it to put forth the effort to overcome any inherent resistance to gratitude.

There is a story about a blind man who was begging in a city park. Someone approached and asked him whether people were giving generously. The blind man shook a nearly empty tin.

The visitor said to him, "Let me write something on your card." The blind man agreed.

Several hours later, the visitor returned, and the blind man showed him a tin full of money and asked, "What on Earth did you write on my card?"

"Oh," the visitor said, "I merely wrote, 'Today is a spring day, and I am blind.'"

The coins people put into the blind man's cup were expressions of gratitude for their ability to see a beautiful spring day.

To be a spiritual person, you need to find ways to live in gratitude.

Now it's your turn. Consider the character trait you want to change, the one you wrote down in step 3. Where might you begin to make a change? In your journal, rewrite these sentences, filling in the blanks as you go.

The trait I want to change is:

I will begin the change today by:

My goal for this week will be to:

Gradually, my goal is to change this trait to:

Remember, spiritual acts tend to bring about other spiritual acts. So even though you are working on one trait at a time, don't be surprised if other things begin improving at the same time!

Step 5

"I will cultivate enjoyable spiritual experiences."

Some people are under the impression that spirituality detracts from enjoyment of life. Nothing can be further from the truth. There are myriad ways you can have an enjoyable spiritual experience. The purpose of step 5 is not only to identify what you *might* do to experience more pleasure but also to *carry it out*!

In case you need a little inspiration, here are a few suggestions:

Go to a forest and look up at the tall trees that seem to touch the sky. Ponder the majesty of the trees. How did they get that way? You might think about the marvels of God's creation. Or you might think about the intricate changes that occurred many centuries ago to bring these trees into existence.

Go to the planetarium and enjoy the show. Think about the billions of stars out there in galaxies that are millions of light-years away. Do you know how much a light-year is? Light travels at 186,000 miles *per second*. The nearest star to Earth is four light-years away, which is 20,878,000,000,000 miles away! This number is so great that it is practically meaningless because we have no experience with distances like this. Now think of a galaxy that is a million times farther than that, and that's only the part of the universe that our telescopes have been able to reach.

Look through a microscope at the structure of a leaf. You probably see thousands of leaves every day without really "seeing" them. Study the intricate structure of a leaf, and you'll realize that it is a greater marvel than the Golden Gate Bridge. That is a spiritual experience.

Help another person. When you mow the lawn for your father, that is a spiritual act. Observing Mother's Day is a spiritual act (although it is much more spiritual if you show gratitude toward your mother the other 364 days). Giving extra attention to your children, or helping a friend in need, or lending a hand to a coworker—these are spiritual acts.

If you are not in a position to help someone, empathizing with him or her is also a spiritual act. People in distress may feel alone and abandoned. Just knowing that someone feels their distress can be comforting.

Reading a history book can be a spiritual act. As you learn about the mighty Egyptian, Greek, and Roman empires, if you enjoy reading history, you are enjoying spirituality.

One person told me that he contributes to a fund that gives children with fatal diseases a chance to fulfill a wish. He has a little collection box in his bedroom, and the first thing he does every morning is put a coin into the box. "It makes me start my day right."

The world is full of things you can enjoy in a spiritual way. In your journal, jot down some ideas of what you might do today ... this week ... this month. It is important to keep these activities manageable (that is, not something that will require more time or money or effort than you have to give) because, as I said at the outset, it is important that you actually *do* it! What will bring you spiritual pleasure?

Step 6

"I will give serious consideration to the relative importance of things."

There are things that are important, and then there are things that are *really* important.

I once received a call from a police sergeant in a university town not too far from Pittsburgh. An eighteen-year-old student had been arrested for "streaking." The sergeant felt that the young man had a psychiatric problem, and the sergeant was willing to release the young man with no charges if he could be admitted to a psychiatric hospital. I told the sergeant that I would gladly admit him. The sergeant said he would contact the father to come for the young man.

This young man's father happened to be the chairman of the board of a major corporation and was in New York at the time, presiding at an annual stockholders' meeting. He could not come for his son for two days, and the young man remained in jail until his father got there.

Several years later, I heard that the young man had committed suicide. I could not help but wonder whether the father's attitude that a stockholders' meeting took priority over getting his son out of jail and into a hospital might have contributed to the young man's disillusionment and depression.

Compare this to the case of an internationally renowned physician who is my host whenever I lecture in his city. On one visit he said,

"I'm glad to be able to see you, Abe. I was supposed to be away this week for lectures in Cairo and China. But I found out that this is the last game of the football season. Jeff is on the team, and I know he wants me in the stands when he plays."

I was thrilled. This physician cancelled his lectures at two important international conferences because something more important had come up: his son's football game.

A spiritual person prioritizes correctly.

To initiate step 6, create three lists in your journal: (1) your priorities for today; (2) your priorities for this week; and (3) your priorities for this year. Don't try to make the "perfect" list; just jot down what comes to your mind right now. You can always come back and refine your lists later.

Below is a sample of what I mean. (All of these are important, and you may be able to get them all done, but just in case you can't, number which are most important to you.)

1. Things I should do today:
    • go to the office and process the daily work
    • meet Sandra for lunch (it's her birthday)
    • buy Sandra a birthday gift
    • attend the school board meeting
    • watch the play-off game
    • take the car in for inspection
    • talk with the kids about how their day was in school
    • ask the water company to recheck the meter
    • call the building manager about the air-conditioning in the office

2. What I'd like to get done this week:
    • finish the monthly report so I can review it before the next executive committee meeting
    • keep my promise to Ed to help him paint his garage

- meet with a new marketing firm
- have my vision rechecked for new glasses
- help Sandra's mother with her tax return
- return the overdue library books
- replace the air-conditioning filters
- attend the Kiwanis Club meeting

3. What I'd like to achieve this year:
  - reduce my indebtedness
  - give the kids an enjoyable vacation trip
  - finish the course work for re-credentialing
  - try to get Sandra back on talking terms with Estelle
  - help Jim with his search for a college
  - lose thirty pounds

This is a very beneficial exercise to help you look at the relative importance of things in your life. It can be even more helpful if you review your lists in a week. What has shifted? Are the things you listed last week as "priority" still priorities? What does this tell you about the relative importance of these events? What does this suggest about how you want to allocate your time and energy?

Step 7

*"I will avoid things that are inimical
to my spirituality."*

We live in a materialistic society that is driven by the desire for economic gain, and some commercial practices are definitely antithetical to spirituality. It's no secret that the entertainment industry capitalizes on the base human traits. Many television programs spew violence and lewdness, and it has been proven beyond a doubt that exposure to these programs increases violent behavior and sexual assaults. The violent electronic games that are marketed to children are unconscionable.

There are also many things that hinder spirituality more subtly. Think of "fuzz-busters." You know—the radar detectors that can prevent you from being caught speeding. Have you ever thought about the fact that this apparatus sends this message to children: "It's okay to break the law, as long as you make sure you don't get caught."

Think of the subtle (or, sometimes, not-so-subtle!) influences of the commercial world that try to convince us that we *have* to have the latest thing. In his book *The Rhythm of Life*, Matthew Kelly describes hearing a lecture on marketing in which the professor said, "Marketing is about creating needs in consumers. It's about creating a desire in people that, in turn, makes them feel that they need your product or service. It's about making people feel they need things even if they don't."

Kelly was stunned, not only by the professor's words, but even more by the attitude of the students who accepted the idea of exploiting people's weaknesses for their own gain as proper behavior.

The goal of step 7 is to increase your alertness to the forces in our culture that are antithetical to your spiritual values, and then to consider what you want to do to protect yourself—and your children—from these influences.

In your journal, make a list of influences that seem to hinder your spiritual life. For each one, note what you might do to counter or avoid this influence.

Step 8

"I will laugh more."

I am convinced that laughing is not only a trait unique to humans, and therefore a component of the spirit, but also that it is therapeutic. There are many studies to support that a hearty laugh is conducive to recovery. I often advise patients with serious illnesses to get comedy videos, even slapstick humor.

I once asked several patients with cancer to trade a joke with me every day. I would fax a joke to them, and they would fax one to me. At the very least, this small effort picked up their spirits, and they were able to function better.

I remember a psychiatrist whom I met at a convention. Sitting across the table from him, I noticed that he periodically would put his thumb and forefinger to his mouth and raise the corners of his mouth as though he were smiling. The psychiatrist noted my curiosity and said, "I believe that smiling is healthy. Even if one does not have the emotion, I think there is something in the movement of the facial muscles when one smiles that is beneficial. I don't have much to smile about today, so I move the muscles of smiling manually."

If you are thinking this is far-fetched, consider this report by a doctor who injected a muscle-paralyzing chemical into the muscles of the lower forehead that made it impossible to frown. He reported great success in relieving depression with this treatment. Apparently, just the muscular activity of a frown can depress a person!

If you're a person who laughs easily, and a lot, step 8 may be natural for you. But if you're a person who takes life pretty seriously, or whose work leaves little time for laughter and lightheartedness, this is a step that could make a big difference in how you live and how happy you are. Similar to my recommendation to the cancer patients, I suggest any or all of the following:

- Tell one joke a day
- Ask someone to tell you one joke a day
- Choose one common occurrence (such as a phone ringing) as a signal to smile each time you hear or see it (whether you *feel* like smiling or not)
- Plan one thing to do each week that will generate laughter
- Seek out people who are "laughers"
- Ask a friend to help you laugh more

Your "I want to laugh more" list will be unique to you. In your journal, write your intentions to increase the laughter quotient in your life. Keep a log of how the increase in laughter affects you—and those around you.

Step 9

"I will work to keep setbacks
from discouraging me."

Spiritual growth is rarely a smooth ascent. There are many "slips" along the way. But rather than be discouragements, they can be learning experiences.

One subzero winter day, I needed to mail a letter at the post office. My car would not start, but since the post office was just several blocks away, I decided to walk. I knew that there were icy patches, so I proceeded cautiously. However, despite my careful steps, I slipped and fell. I got up and walked the rest of the way (no fractures, just bruises), but this time I was much more cautious.

This incident taught me two things. First, although I had fallen, I was still two blocks closer to my destination. I was not back at home. The two blocks of progress before the fall could not be taken from me. Second, I realized that what I had thought was adequate caution was, in fact, not enough. I learned that I needed to be more alert.

This is equally true of spirituality. If you are able, for example, to keep from flying into a rage when provoked three times in a row but lose your temper the fourth time, that does not take away from the progress you have made. The last incident notwithstanding, you are still in a much better condition to manage your anger than you had originally been. Furthermore, you are in a position to analyze this fourth incident and see what kept you from being able to control your angry reaction. What you learn will help you avoid similar reactions in the future.

This is where keeping a journal record can be extremely valuable. When you experience a setback, rather than giving in to discouragement, use your journal to help you analyze what went wrong and what you might learn about yourself from the situation. Then consider what you will do differently the next time. Having this written record will not only help you stay on track in the future, but it will also help you see the progress you have made.

Step 10

"I realize there is never an end
to spiritual growth."

It has been said that we have spirituality only as long as we are striving to achieve it. If we think we have already achieved it, then we've lost it.

Since no human being is ever without shortcomings, there is no limit to how much we can refine our character. Paradoxically, our attempts to improve, to be the best we can be, will likely reveal more character defects. Think of it this way: a tiny spot on a coarse garment may hardly be noticeable. The same tiny spot on a fine silk garment would be very conspicuous.

As you advance spiritually, character traits that you may not have considered shortcomings in the past might now show up as conspicuous stains on your character. In other words, the more spiritual you become, the more sensitive you will be to things that you want to improve.

The truth is that step 10 never ends. You will never "graduate" from the University of Spirituality, and that is a good thing. As long as you are a student who is always learning about yourself and how you can improve yourself, you will always be moving toward being a happier person.

Epilogue

Throughout history, many philosophical systems and disciplines—religion, psychology, psychiatry, philosophy, even nonreligious and antireligious systems—have tried to explain and aid the human struggle for mastery over mind and behavior. At first, there does not appear to be a common denominator to all these systems. Religion may conflict with psychology, communism may conflict with religion, and so forth.

Enter *spirituality*, and the common denominator becomes apparent. There may be differences of opinion about *what* the optimum for human beings to be is, but any system can advocate that people become the best they can be.

The concept is simple. Every living creature comes into the world in a state of potentiality. Except for human beings, nature has endowed every creature with the instincts that can lead to its actualization. We humans are the exception. In order to become the best we can be, we need to focus our efforts in that direction, to intentionally exercise and implement the traits of the human spirit to the best of our abilities. This process—whether we call it actualization, self-improvement, personal growth, or self-fulfillment—is *spirituality*. Failure to embrace spirituality leaves us in a state of incompleteness and discontent.

Our happiness depends on being complete people. We are not born violinists, engineers, doctors, or scientists. Though we may excel in any of these occupations, perfecting ourselves as human beings lies not in a skill, but in maximizing ourselves in every way possible.

I hope this exploration of what it means to be a spiritual person will help you achieve the happiness that is your "unalienable right" and help you become the person you were created to be.

Suggestions for
Further Reading

Adiswarananda, Swami. *The Vedanta Way to Peace and Happiness.* Woodstock, VT: SkyLight Paths, 2004, and New York: Ramakrishna-Vivekananda Center, 2004.

Branden, Nathaniel. *How to Raise Your Self-Esteem.* New York: Bantam, 1987.

———. *Six Pillars of Self-Esteem.* New York: Bantam, 1994.

Canfield, Jack, et al. *Chicken Soup for the Couple's Soul.* Deerfield Beach, FL: Health Communications, Inc., 1999.

———. *Chicken Soup for the Girl's Soul.* Deerfield Beach, FL: Health Communications, Inc., 2005.

———. *Chicken Soup for the Grandparent's Soul.* Deerfield Beach, FL: Health Communications, Inc., 2004.

———. *Chicken Soup for the Prisoner's Soul.* Deerfield Beach, FL: Health Communications, Inc., 2002.

———. *Chicken Soup for the Recovering Soul.* Deerfield Beach, FL: Health Communications, Inc., 2004.

———. *Chicken Soup for the Teenage Soul.* Deerfield Beach, FL: Health Communications., Inc., 1997.

———. *Living Your Dreams.* Deerfield Beach, FL: Health Communications, Inc., 2003.

Chopra, Deepak. *The Seven Spiritual Laws of Success.* Novato, CA: New World Library, 1994.

Clarke, Jean Illsley. *Self-Esteem: A Family Affair.* Center City, MN: Hazelden, 1998.

Frankl, Viktor. *Man's Search for Meaning.* (Written in 1945 and first published in English, by Beacon Press, in 1959; many editions have been released since then.)

Gill, Brendan. *Late Bloomers.* New York: Workman/Artisan, 1998.

Gough, Russell. *Character Is Destiny.* New York: Crown Forum, 1997.

Hammarskjöld, Dag. *Markings.* New York: Ballantine, 1964.

Kedar, Karyn D. *The Bridge to Forgiveness: Stories and Prayers for Finding God and Restoring Wholeness.* Woodstock, VT: Jewish Lights, 2007.

————. *God Whispers: Stories of the Soul, Lessons of the Heart.* Woodstock, VT: Jewish Lights, 2000.

————. *Our Dance with God: Finding Prayer, Perspective and Meaning in the Stories of Our Lives.* Woodstock, VT: Jewish Lights, 2004.

Kelly, Matthew. *The Rhythm of Life.* New York: Simon and Schuster, 1999.

Kurtz, Ernest, and Katherine Ketcham. *The Spirituality of Imperfection.* New York: Bantam Books, 1992.

Lapsley, Daniel K., and F. Clark Power. *Character Psychology and Character Education.* Notre Dame, IN: University of Notre Dame Press, 2005.

Remen, Rachel Naomi. *Kitchen Table Wisdom.* New York: Riverhead Books, 1996.

————. *My Grandfather's Blessings.* New York: Riverhead Books, 2000.

Shapiro, Rami. *The Sacred Art of Lovingkindness: Preparing to Practice.* Woodstock, VT: SkyLight Paths, 2006.

Twerski, Abraham J. *The Spiritual Self.* Center City, MN: Hazelden, 2000.

Bible Study/Midrash

Ancient Secrets: Using the Stories of the Bible to Improve Our Everyday Lives
By Rabbi Levi Meier, PhD 5½ x 8½, 288 pp, Quality PB, 978-1-58023-064-3 **$16.95**

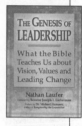

The Genesis of Leadership: What the Bible Teaches Us about Vision,
Values and Leading Change *By Rabbi Nathan Laufer; Foreword by Senator Joseph I. Lieberman*
Unlike other books on leadership, this one is rooted in the stories of the Bible, and
teaches the values that the Bible believes are prerequisites for true leadership.
6 x 9, 288 pp, HC, 978-1-58023-241-8 **$24.99**

Hineini in Our Lives: Learning How to Respond to Others through 14 Biblical Texts and
Personal Stories *By Norman J. Cohen* 6 x 9, 240 pp, Quality PB, 978-1-58023-274-6 **$16.99**

Moses and the Journey to Leadership: Timeless Lessons of Effective Management from
the Bible and Today's Leaders *By Dr. Norman J. Cohen* 6 x 9, 250 pp, HC, 978-1-58023-227-2 **$21.99**

Self, Struggle & Change: Family Conflict Stories in Genesis and Their Healing Insights for
Our Lives *By Norman J. Cohen* 6 x 9, 224 pp, Quality PB, 978-1-879045-66-8 **$18.99**

The Triumph of Eve & Other Subversive Bible Tales *By Matt Biers-Ariel*
5½ x 8½, 192 pp, Quality PB, 978-1-59473-176-1 **$14.99**; HC, 978-1-59473-040-5 **$19.99**
(A SkyLight Paths book)

Voices from Genesis: Guiding Us through the Stages of Life *By Norman J. Cohen*
6 x 9, 192 pp, Quality PB, 978-1-58023-118-3 **$16.95**

Children's Books

What You Will See Inside a Synagogue
By Rabbi Lawrence A. Hoffman and Dr. Ron Wolfson; Full-color photos by Bill Aron
A colorful, fun-to-read introduction that explains the ways and whys of Jewish
worship and religious life.
8½ x 10½, 32 pp, Full-color photos, HC, 978-1-59473-012-2 **$17.99** *For ages 6 & up (A SkyLight Paths book)*

In God's Hands
By Lawrence Kushner and Gary Schmidt 9 x 12, 32 pp, HC, 978-1-58023-224-1 **$16.99**

Because Nothing Looks Like God
By Lawrence and Karen Kushner
Introduces children to the possibilities of spiritual life.
11 x 8½, 32 pp, Full-color illus., HC, 978-1-58023-092-6 **$16.95** *For ages 4 & up*

Also Available: **Because Nothing Looks Like God Teacher's Guide**
8½ x 11, 22 pp, PB, 978-1-58023-140-4 **$6.95** *For ages 5–8*

> **Board Book Companions** to *Because Nothing Looks Like God*
> 5 x 5, 24 pp, Full-color illus., SkyLight Paths Board Books *For ages 0–4*

What Does God Look Like? 978-1-893361-23-2 **$7.99**

How Does God Make Things Happen? 978-1-893361-24-9 **$7.95**

Where Is God? 978-1-893361-17-1 **$7.99**

The Book of Miracles: A Young Person's Guide to Jewish Spiritual Awareness
By Lawrence Kushner. All-new illustrations by the author
6 x 9, 96 pp, 2-color illus., HC, 978-1-879045-78-1 **$16.95** *For ages 9 and up*

In Our Image: God's First Creatures
By Nancy Sohn Swartz 9 x 12, 32 pp, Full-color illus., HC, 978-1-879045-99-6 **$16.95** *For ages 4 & up*

Also Available as a Board Book: **How Did the Animals Help God?**
5 x 5, 24 pp, Board, Full-color illus., 978-1-59473-044-3 **$7.99** *For ages 0–4 (A SkyLight Paths book)*

Or phone, fax, mail or e-mail to: **JEWISH LIGHTS Publishing**
Sunset Farm Offices, Route 4 • P.O. Box 237 • Woodstock, Vermont 05091
Tel: (802) 457-4000 • Fax: (802) 457-4004 • www.jewishlights.com
Credit card orders: (800) 962-4544 (8:30AM–5:30PM ET Monday–Friday)
Generous discounts on quantity orders. SATISFACTION GUARANTEED. Prices subject to change.

Children's Books
by Sandy Eisenberg Sasso

Adam & Eve's First Sunset: God's New Day

Engaging new story explores fear and hope, faith and gratitude in ways that will delight kids and adults—inspiring us to bless each of God's days and nights.

9 x 12, 32 pp, Full-color illus., HC, 978-1-58023-177-0 **$17.95** *For ages 4 & up*

Also Available as a Board Book: **Adam and Eve's New Day**

5 x 5, 24 pp, Full-color illus., Board, 978-1-59473-205-8 **$7.99** *For ages 0–4 (A SkyLight Paths book)*

But God Remembered

Stories of Women from Creation to the Promised Land

Four different stories of women—Lillith, Serach, Bityah, and the Daughters of Z—teach us important values through their faith and actions.

9 x 12, 32 pp, Full-color illus., HC, 978-1-879045-43-9 **$16.95** *For ages 8 & up*

Cain & Abel: Finding the Fruits of Peace

Shows children that we have the power to deal with anger in positive ways. Provides questions for kids and adults to explore together.

9 x 12, 32 pp, Full-color illus., HC, 978-1-58023-123-7 **$16.95** *For ages 5 & up*

God in Between

If you wanted to find God, where would you look? This magical, mythical tale teaches that God can be found where we are: within all of us and the relationships between us.

9 x 12, 32 pp, Full-color illus., HC, 978-1-879045-86-6 **$16.95** *For ages 4 & up*

God's Paintbrush: Special 10th Anniversary Edition

Wonderfully interactive, invites children of all faiths and backgrounds to encounter God through moments in their own lives. Provides questions adult and child can explore together.

11 x 8½, 32 pp, Full-color illus., HC, 978-1-58023-195-4 **$17.95** *For ages 4 & up*

Also Available: **God's Paintbrush Teacher's Guide**

8½ x 11, 32 pp, PB, 978-1-879045-57-6 **$8.95**

God's Paintbrush Celebration Kit

A Spiritual Activity Kit for Teachers and Students of All Faiths, All Backgrounds
Additional activity sheets available:
8-Student Activity Sheet Pack (40 sheets/5 sessions), 978-1-58023-058-2 **$19.95**
Single-Student Activity Sheet Pack (5 sessions), 978-1-58023-059-9 **$3.95**

In God's Name

Like an ancient myth in its poetic text and vibrant illustrations, this award-winning modern fable about the search for God's name celebrates the diversity and, at the same time, the unity of all people.

9 x 12, 32 pp, Full-color illus., HC, 978-1-879045-26-2 **$16.99** *For ages 4 & up*

Also Available as a Board Book: **What Is God's Name?**

5 x 5, 24 pp, Board, Full-color illus., 978-1-893361-10-2 **$7.99** *For ages 0–4 (A SkyLight Paths book)*

Also Available: **In God's Name video and study guide**

Computer animation, original music, and children's voices. 18 min. **$29.99**

Also Available in Spanish: **El nombre de Dios**

9 x 12, 32 pp, Full-color illus., HC, 978-1-893361-63-8 **$16.95** *(A SkyLight Paths book)*

Noah's Wife: The Story of Naamah

When God tells Noah to bring the animals of the world onto the ark, God also calls on Naamah, Noah's wife, to save each plant on Earth. Based on an ancient text.

9 x 12, 32 pp, Full-color illus., HC, 978-1-58023-134-3 **$16.95** *For ages 4 & up*

Also Available as a Board Book: **Naamah, Noah's Wife**

5 x 5, 24 pp, Full-color illus., Board, 978-1-893361-56-0 **$7.95** *For ages 0–4 (A SkyLight Paths book)*

For Heaven's Sake: Finding God in Unexpected Places

9 x 12, 32 pp, Full-color illus., HC, 978-1-58023-054-4 **$16.95** *For ages 4 & up*

God Said Amen: Finding the Answers to Our Prayers

9 x 12, 32 pp, Full-color illus., HC, 978-1-58023-080-3 **$16.95** *For ages 4 & up*

Current Events/History

The Story of the Jews: A 4,000-Year Adventure—A Graphic History Book
Written & illustrated by Stan Mack
Witty, illustrated narrative of all the major happenings from biblical times to the twenty-first century. 6 x 9, 288 pp, illus., Quality PB, 978-1-58023-155-8 **$16.95**

Hannah Senesh: Her Life and Diary, the First Complete Edition
By Hannah Senesh; Foreword by Marge Piercy; Preface by Eitan Senesh
6 x 9, 352 pp, HC, 978-1-58023-212-8 **$24.99**

The Jewish Prophet: Visionary Words from Moses and Miriam to Henrietta Szold
and A. J. Heschel *By Rabbi Dr. Michael J. Shire*
6½ x 8½, 128 pp, 123 full-color illus., HC, 978-1-58023-168-8
Special gift price $14.95

Foundations of Sephardic Spirituality: The Inner Life of Jews of the Ottoman Empire
By Rabbi Marc D. Angel, PhD 6 x 9, 224 pp, HC, 978-1-58023-243-2 **$24.99**

Judaism and Justice: The Jewish Passion to Repair the World
By Rabbi Sidney Schwarz
6 x 9, 250 pp, HC, 978-1-58023-312-5 **$24.99**

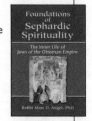

Ecology

Ecology & the Jewish Spirit: Where Nature & the Sacred Meet
Edited by Ellen Bernstein 6 x 9, 288 pp, Quality PB, 978-1-58023-082-7 **$16.95**

Torah of the Earth: Exploring 4,000 Years of Ecology in Jewish Thought
Vol. 1: Biblical Israel: One Land, One People; Rabbinic Judaism: One People, Many Lands
Vol. 2: Zionism: One Land, Two Peoples; Eco-Judaism: One Earth, Many Peoples
Edited by Arthur Waskow
Vol. 1: 6 x 9, 272 pp, Quality PB, 978-1-58023-086-5 **$19.95**
Vol. 2: 6 x 9, 336 pp, Quality PB, 978-1-58023-087-2 **$19.95**

The Way Into Judaism and the Environment
By Jeremy Benstein 6 x 9, 224 pp, HC, 978-1-58023-268-5 **$24.99**

Grief/Healing

Against the Dying of the Light: A Parent's Story of Love, Loss and Hope
By Leonard Fein
5½ x 8½, 176 pp, Quality PB, 978-1-58023-197-8 **$15.99**

Grief in Our Seasons: A Mourner's Kaddish Companion *By Rabbi Kerry M. Olitzky*
4½ x 6½, 448 pp, Quality PB, 978-1-879045-55-2 **$15.95**

Healing of Soul, Healing of Body: Spiritual Leaders Unfold the Strength & Solace
in Psalms *Edited by Rabbi Simkha Y. Weintraub, CSW*
6 x 9, 128 pp, 2-color illus. text, Quality PB, 978-1-879045-31-6 **$14.99**

Jewish Paths toward Healing and Wholeness: A Personal Guide to Dealing with
Suffering *By Rabbi Kerry M. Olitzky; Foreword by Debbie Friedman.*
6 x 9, 192 pp, Quality PB, 978-1-58023-068-1 **$15.95**

Mourning & Mitzvah, 2nd Edition: A Guided Journal for Walking the Mourner's
Path through Grief to Healing *By Anne Brener, LCSW*
7½ x 9, 304 pp, Quality PB, 978-1-58023-113-8 **$19.99**

The Perfect Stranger's Guide to Funerals and Grieving Practices
A Guide to Etiquette in Other People's Religious Ceremonies *Edited by Stuart M. Matlins*
6 x 9, 240 pp, Quality PB, 978-1-893361-20-1 **$16.95** *(A SkyLight Paths book)*

Tears of Sorrow, Seeds of Hope, 2nd Edition: A Jewish Spiritual Companion for
Infertility and Pregnancy Loss *By Rabbi Nina Beth Cardin*
6 x 9, 208 pp, Quality PB, 978-1-58023-233-3 **$18.99**

A Time to Mourn, A Time to Comfort, 2nd Edition: A Guide to Jewish
Bereavement *By Dr. Ron Wolfson*
7 x 9, 384 pp, Quality PB, 978-1-58023-253-1 **$19.99**

When a Grandparent Dies: A Kid's Own Remembering Workbook for Dealing
with Shiva and the Year Beyond *By Nechama Liss-Levinson, PhD*
8 x 10, 48 pp, 2-color text, HC, 978-1-879045-44-6 **$15.95** *For ages 7–13*

Theology/Philosophy

Christians and Jews in Dialogue: Learning in the Presence of the Other
By Mary C. Boys and Sara S. Lee; Foreword by Dr. Dorothy Bass
6 x 9, 240 pp, HC, 978-1-59473-144-0 **$21.99** *(A SkyLight Paths book)*

The Death of Death: Resurrection and Immortality in Jewish Thought
By Neil Gillman 6 x 9, 336 pp, Quality PB, 978-1-58023-081-0 **$18.95**

Ethics of the Sages: Pirke Avot—Annotated & Explained
Translation & Annotation by Rabbi Rami Shapiro
5½ x 8½, 208 pp, Quality PB, 978-1-59473-207-2 **$16.99** *(A SkyLight Paths book)*

Evolving Halakhah: A Progressive Approach to Traditional Jewish Law
By Rabbi Dr. Moshe Zemer 6 x 9, 480 pp, Quality PB, 978-1-58023-127-5 **$29.95**;
HC, 978-1-58023-002-5 **$40.00**

Hasidic Tales: Annotated & Explained
By Rabbi Rami Shapiro; Foreword by Andrew Harvey
5½ x 8½, 240 pp, Quality PB, 978-1-893361-86-7 **$16.95** *(A SkyLight Paths Book)*

Healing the Jewish-Christian Rift: Growing Beyond our Wounded History
By Ron Miller and Laura Bernstein; Foreword by Dr. Beatrice Bruteau
6 x 9, 288 pp, Quality PB, 978-1-59473-139-6 **$18.99** *(A SkyLight Paths book)*

A Heart of Many Rooms: Celebrating the Many Voices within Judaism
By David Hartman 6 x 9, 352 pp, Quality PB, 978-1-58023-156-5 **$19.95**

The Hebrew Prophets: Selections Annotated & Explained
Translation & Annotation by Rabbi Rami Shapiro; Foreword by Zalman M. Schachter-Shalomi
5½ x 8½, 224 pp, Quality PB, 978-1-59473-037-5 **$16.99** *(A SkyLight Paths book)*

A Jewish Understanding of the New Testament
By Rabbi Samuel Sandmel; Preface by Rabbi David Sandmel
5½ x 8½, 368 pp, Quality PB, 978-1-59473-048-1 **$19.99** *(A SkyLight Paths book)*

Keeping Faith with the Psalms: Deepen Your Relationship with God Using the Book
of Psalms *By Daniel F. Polish* 6 x 9, 320 pp, Quality PB, 978-1-58023-300-2 **$18.99**;
HC, 978-1-58023-179-4 **$24.95**

A Living Covenant: The Innovative Spirit in Traditional Judaism
By David Hartman 6 x 9, 368 pp, Quality PB, 978-1-58023-011-7 **$20.00**

Love and Terror in the God Encounter
The Theological Legacy of Rabbi Joseph B. Soloveitchik
By David Hartman 6 x 9, 240 pp, Quality PB, 978-1-58023-176-3 **$19.95**;
HC, 978-1-58023-112-1 **$25.00**

The Personhood of God: Biblical Theology, Human Faith and the Divine Image
By Dr. Yochanan Muffs; Foreword by Dr. David Hartman
6 x 9, 240 pp, HC, 978-1-58023-265-4 **$24.99**

Tormented Master: The Life and Spiritual Quest of Rabbi Nahman of Bratslav
By Arthur Green 6 x 9, 416 pp, Quality PB, 978-1-879045-11-8 **$19.99**

Traces of God: Seeing God in Torah, History and Everyday Life
By Neil Gillman 6 x 9, 240 pp, HC, 978-1-58023-249-4 **$21.99**

We Jews and Jesus: Exploring Theological Differences for Mutual Understanding
By Rabbi Samuel Sandmel; Preface by Rabbi David Sandmel
6 x 9, 176 pp, Quality PB, 978-1-59473-208-9 **$16.99** *(A SkyLight Paths book)*

Your Word Is Fire: The Hasidic Masters on Contemplative Prayer
Edited and translated by Arthur Green and Barry W. Holtz
6 x 9, 160 pp, Quality PB, 978-1-879045-25-5 **$15.95**

I Am Jewish

Personal Reflections Inspired by the Last Words of Daniel Pearl

Almost 150 Jews—both famous and not—from all walks of life, from all around
the world, write about Identity, Heritage, Covenant / Chosenness and Faith,
Humanity and Ethnicity, and *Tikkun Olam* and Justice.
Edited by Judea and Ruth Pearl
6 x 9, 304 pp, Deluxe PB w/flaps, 978-1-58023-259-3 **$18.99**; HC, 978-1-58023-183-1 **$24.99**
**Download a free copy of the *I Am Jewish Teacher's Guide* at our website:
www.jewishlights.com**

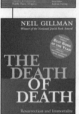

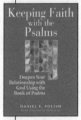

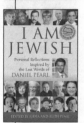

Meditation

The Handbook of Jewish Meditation Practices
A Guide for Enriching the Sabbath and Other Days of Your Life
By Rabbi David A. Cooper Easy-to-learn meditation techniques.
6 x 9, 208 pp, Quality PB, 978-1-58023-102-2 **$16.95**

Discovering Jewish Meditation: Instruction & Guidance for Learning an Ancient
Spiritual Practice *By Nan Fink Gefen*
6 x 9, 208 pp, Quality PB, 978-1-58023-067-4 **$16.95**

A Heart of Stillness: A Complete Guide to Learning the Art of Meditation
By David A. Cooper 5½ x 8½, 272 pp, Quality PB, 978-1-893361-03-4 **$16.95** *(A SkyLight Paths book)*

Meditation from the Heart of Judaism: Today's Teachers Share Their
Practices, Techniques, and Faith *Edited by Avram Davis*
6 x 9, 256 pp, Quality PB, 978-1-58023-049-0 **$16.95**

Silence, Simplicity & Solitude: A Complete Guide to Spiritual Retreat at Home
By David A. Cooper 5½ x 8½, 336 pp, Quality PB, 978-1-893361-04-1 **$16.95**
(A SkyLight Paths book)

The Way of Flame: A Guide to the Forgotten Mystical Tradition of Jewish
Meditation *By Avram Davis* 4½ x 8, 176 pp, Quality PB, 978-1-58023-060-5 **$15.95**

Ritual/Sacred Practice/Journaling

The Jewish Dream Book: The Key to Opening the Inner Meaning of
Your Dreams *By Vanessa L. Ochs with Elizabeth Ochs; Full-color illus. by Kristina Swarner*
Instructions for how modern people can perform ancient Jewish dream practices
and dream interpretations drawn from the Jewish wisdom tradition.
8 x 8, 128 pp, Full-color illus., Deluxe PB w/flaps, 978-1-58023-132-9 **$16.95**

The Jewish Journaling Book: How to Use Jewish Tradition to Write
Your Life & Explore Your Soul *By Janet Ruth Falon*
Details the history of Jewish journaling throughout biblical and modern times, and
teaches specific journaling techniques to help you create and maintain a vital journal,
from a Jewish perspective. 8 x 8, 304 pp, Deluxe PB w/flaps, 978-1-58023-203-6 **$18.99**

The Book of Jewish Sacred Practices: CLAL's Guide to Everyday & Holiday
Rituals & Blessings *Edited by Rabbi Irwin Kula and Vanessa L. Ochs, PhD*
6 x 9, 368 pp, Quality PB, 978-1-58023-152-7 **$18.95**

Jewish Ritual: A Brief Introduction for Christians
By Rabbi Kerry M. Olitzky and Rabbi Daniel Judson
5½ x 8½, 144 pp, Quality PB, 978-1-58023-210-4 **$14.99**

The Rituals & Practices of a Jewish Life: A Handbook for Personal Spiritual
Renewal *Edited by Rabbi Kerry M. Olitzky and Rabbi Daniel Judson*
6 x 9, 272 pp, illus., Quality PB, 978-1-58023-169-5 **$18.95**

The Sacred Art of Lovingkindness: Preparing to Practice
By Rabbi Rami Shapiro 5½ x 8½, 176 pp, Quality PB, 978-1-59473-151-8 **$16.99**
(A SkyLight Paths book)

Science Fiction/Mystery & Detective Fiction

Mystery Midrash: An Anthology of Jewish Mystery & Detective Fiction
Edited by Lawrence W. Raphael; Preface by Joel Siegel
6 x 9, 304 pp, Quality PB, 978-1-58023-055-1 **$16.95**

Criminal Kabbalah: An Intriguing Anthology of Jewish Mystery & Detective Fiction
Edited by Lawrence W. Raphael; Foreword by Laurie R. King
6 x 9, 256 pp, Quality PB, 978-1-58023-109-1 **$16.95**

Wandering Stars: An Anthology of Jewish Fantasy & Science Fiction
Edited by Jack Dann; Introduction by Isaac Asimov
6 x 9, 272 pp, Quality PB, 978-1-58023-005-6 **$16.95**

More Wandering Stars: An Anthology of Outstanding Stories of Jewish Fantasy and
Science Fiction *Edited by Jack Dann; Introduction by Isaac Asimov*
6 x 9, 192 pp, Quality PB, 978-1-58023-063-6 **$16.95**

Spirituality/Lawrence Kushner

Filling Words with Light: Hasidic and Mystical Reflections on Jewish Prayer
By Lawrence Kushner and Nehemia Polen
5½ x 8½, 176 pp, HC, 978-1-58023-216-6 **$21.99**

The Book of Letters: A Mystical Hebrew Alphabet
Popular HC Edition, 6 x 9, 80 pp, 2-color text, 978-1-879045-00-2 **$24.95**
Collector's Limited Edition, 9 x 12, 80 pp, gold foil embossed pages, w/limited edition silkscreened print, 978-1-879045-04-0 **$349.00**

The Book of Miracles: A Young Person's Guide to Jewish Spiritual Awareness
6 x 9, 96 pp, 2-color illus., HC, 978-1-879045-78-1 **$16.95** *For ages 9 and up*

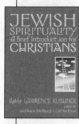

The Book of Words: Talking Spiritual Life, Living Spiritual Talk
6 x 9, 160 pp, Quality PB, 978-1-58023-020-9 **$16.95**

Eyes Remade for Wonder: A Lawrence Kushner Reader *Introduction by Thomas Moore*
6 x 9, 240 pp, Quality PB, 978-1-58023-042-1 **$18.95**

God Was in This Place & I, i Did Not Know: Finding Self, Spirituality and Ultimate Meaning 6 x 9, 192 pp, Quality PB, 978-1-879045-33-0 **$16.95**

Honey from the Rock: An Introduction to Jewish Mysticism
6 x 9, 176 pp, Quality PB, 978-1-58023-073-5 **$16.95**

Invisible Lines of Connection: Sacred Stories of the Ordinary
5½ x 8½, 160 pp, Quality PB, 978-1-879045-98-9 **$15.95**

Jewish Spirituality—A Brief Introduction for Christians
5½ x 8½, 112 pp, Quality PB, 978-1-58023-150-3 **$12.95**

The River of Light: Jewish Mystical Awareness
6 x 9, 192 pp, Quality PB, 978-1-58023-096-4 **$16.95**

The Way Into Jewish Mystical Tradition
6 x 9, 224 pp, Quality PB, 978-1-58023-200-5 **$18.99**; HC, 978-1-58023-029-2 **$21.95**

Spirituality/Prayer

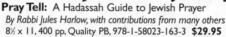
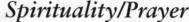

Pray Tell: A Hadassah Guide to Jewish Prayer
By Rabbi Jules Harlow, with contributions from many others
8½ x 11, 400 pp, Quality PB, 978-1-58023-163-3 **$29.95**

Witnesses to the One: The Spiritual History of the *Sh'ma* *By Rabbi Joseph B. Meszler; Foreword by Rabbi Elyse Goldstein* 6 x 9, 176 pp, HC, 978-1-58023-309-5 **$19.99**

My People's Prayer Book Series

Traditional Prayers, Modern Commentaries *Edited by Rabbi Lawrence A. Hoffman*
Provides diverse and exciting commentary to the traditional liturgy, helping modern men and women find new wisdom in Jewish prayer, and bring liturgy into their lives. Each book includes Hebrew text, modern translation, and commentaries from all perspectives of the Jewish world.

Vol. 1—The *Sh'ma* and Its Blessings
7 x 10, 168 pp, HC, 978-1-879045-79-8 **$24.99**
Vol. 2—The *Amidah*
7 x 10, 240 pp, HC, 978-1-879045-80-4 **$24.95**
Vol. 3—*P'sukei D'zimrah* (Morning Psalms)
7 x 10, 240 pp, HC, 978-1-879045-81-1 **$24.95**
Vol. 4—*Seder K'riat Hatorah* (The Torah Service)
7 x 10, 264 pp, HC, 978-1-879045-82-8 **$23.95**
Vol. 5—*Birkhot Hashachar* (Morning Blessings)
7 x 10, 240 pp, HC, 978-1-879045-83-5 **$24.95**
Vol. 6—*Tachanun* and Concluding Prayers
7 x 10, 240 pp, HC, 978-1-879045-84-2 **$24.95**
Vol. 7—Shabbat at Home
7 x 10, 240 pp, HC, 978-1-879045-85-9 **$24.95**
Vol. 8—*Kabbalat Shabbat* (Welcoming Shabbat in the Synagogue)
7 x 10, 240 pp, HC, 978-1-58023-121-3 **$24.99**
Vol. 9—Welcoming the Night: *Minchah* and *Ma'ariv* (Afternoon and Evening Prayer) 7 x 10, 272 pp, HC, 978-1-58023-262-3 **$24.99**
Vol. 10—Shabbat Morning: *Shacharit* and *Musaf* (Morning and Additional Services) 7 x 10, 240 pp, HC, 978-1-58023-240-1 **$24.99**

Spirituality/Women's Interest

The Quotable Jewish Woman: Wisdom, Inspiration & Humor from the Mind & Heart
Edited and compiled by Elaine Bernstein Partnow
6 x 9, 496 pp, Quality PB, 978-1-58023-236-4 **$19.99**; HC, 978-1-58023-193-0 **$29.99**

The Knitting Way: A Guide to Spiritual Self-Discovery *By Linda Skolnick and Janice MacDaniels* 7 x 9, 240 pp, Quality PB, 978-1-59473-079-5 **$16.99** *(A SkyLight Paths book)*

The Quilting Path: A Guide to Spiritual Self-Discovery through Fabric, Thread and Kabbalah
By Louise Silk 7 x 9, 192 pp, Quality PB, 978-1-59473-206-5 **$16.99** *(A SkyLight Paths book)*

The Divine Feminine in Biblical Wisdom Literature: Selections Annotated & Explained *Translated and Annotated by Rabbi Rami Shapiro*
5½ x 8½, 240 pp, Quality PB, 978-1-59473-109-9 **$16.99** *(A SkyLight Paths book)*

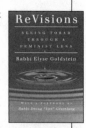

Lifecycles, Vol. 1: Jewish Women on Life Passages & Personal Milestones
Edited and with Introductions by Rabbi Debra Orenstein
6 x 9, 480 pp, Quality PB, 978-1-58023-018-6 **$19.95**

Lifecycles, Vol. 2: Jewish Women on Biblical Themes in Contemporary Life
Edited and with Introductions by Rabbi Debra Orenstein and Rabbi Jane Rachel Litman
6 x 9, 464 pp, Quality PB, 978-1-58023-019-3 **$19.95**

Moonbeams: A Hadassah Rosh Hodesh Guide *Edited by Carol Diament, PhD*
8½ x 11, 240 pp, Quality PB, 978-1-58023-099-5 **$20.00**

ReVisions: Seeing Torah through a Feminist Lens *By Rabbi Elyse Goldstein*
5½ x 8½, 224 pp, Quality PB, 978-1-58023-117-6 **$16.95**

The Women's Haftarah Commentary: New Insights from Women Rabbis on the 54 Weekly Haftarah Portions, the 5 Megillot & Special Shabbatot
Edited by Rabbi Elyse Goldstein 6 x 9, 560 pp, HC, 978-1-58023-133-6 **$39.99**

The Women's Torah Commentary: New Insights from Women Rabbis on the 54 Weekly Torah Portions *Edited by Rabbi Elyse Goldstein*
6 x 9, 496 pp, HC, 978-1-58023-076-6 **$34.95**

The Year Mom Got Religion: One Woman's Midlife Journey into Judaism
By Lee Meyerhoff Hendler 6 x 9, 208 pp, Quality PB, 978-1-58023-070-4 **$15.95**

Travel

Israel—A Spiritual Travel Guide, 2nd Edition
A Companion for the Modern Jewish Pilgrim
By Rabbi Lawrence A. Hoffman 4¾ x 10, 256 pp, Quality PB, illus., 978-1-58023-261-6 **$18.99**
Also Available: **The Israel Mission Leader's Guide** 978-1-58023-085-8 **$4.95**

12-Step

100 Blessings Every Day: Daily Twelve Step Recovery Affirmations, Exercises for Personal Growth & Renewal Reflecting Seasons of the Jewish Year
By Rabbi Kerry M. Olitzky; Foreword by Rabbi Neil Gillman
4½ x 6½, 432 pp, Quality PB, 978-1-879045-30-9 **$15.99**

Recovery from Codependence: A Jewish Twelve Steps Guide to Healing Your Soul
By Rabbi Kerry M. Olitzky 6 x 9, 160 pp, Quality PB, 978-1-879045-32-3 **$13.95**

Renewed Each Day: Daily Twelve Step Recovery Meditations Based on the Bible
By Rabbi Kerry M. Olitzky and Aaron Z.
Vol. 1—Genesis & Exodus: 6 x 9, 224 pp, Quality PB, 978-1-879045-12-5 **$14.95**
Vol. 2—Leviticus, Numbers & Deuteronomy: 6 x 9, 280 pp, Quality PB, 978-1-879045-13-2 **$18.99**

Twelve Jewish Steps to Recovery: A Personal Guide to Turning from Alcoholism & Other Addictions—Drugs, Food, Gambling, Sex ...
By Rabbi Kerry M. Olitzky and Stuart A. Copans, MD; Preface by Abraham J. Twerski, MD
6 x 9, 144 pp, Quality PB, 978-1-879045-09-5 **$14.95**

Spirituality

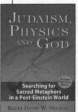

The Adventures of Rabbi Harvey: A Graphic Novel of Jewish Wisdom and Wit in the Wild West *By Steve Sheinkin*
Jewish and American folktales combine in this witty and original graphic novel collection. Creatively retold and set on the western frontier of the 1870s.
6 x 9, 144 pp, Full-color illus., Quality PB, 978-1-58023-310-1 **$16.99**
Also Available: **The Adventures of Rabbi Harvey Teacher's Guide**
8½ x 11, 32 pp, PB, 978-1-58023-326-2 **$8.99**

Ethics of the Sages: Pirke Avot—Annotated & Explained
Translation and Annotation by Rabbi Rami Shapiro
5½ x 8½, 192 pp, Quality PB, 978-1-59473-207-2 **$16.99** *(A SkyLight Paths book)*

A Book of Life: Embracing Judaism as a Spiritual Practice
By Michael Strassfeld 6 x 9, 528 pp, Quality PB, 978-1-58023-247-0 **$19.99**

Meaning and Mitzvah: Daily Practices for Reclaiming Judaism through Prayer, God, Torah, Hebrew, Mitzvot and Peoplehood *By Rabbi Goldie Milgram*
7 x 9, 336 pp, Quality PB, 978-1-58023-256-2 **$19.99**

The Soul of the Story: Meetings with Remarkable People
By Rabbi David Zeller 6 x 9, 288 pp, HC, 978-1-58023-272-2 **$21.99**

Aleph-Bet Yoga: Embodying the Hebrew Letters for Physical and Spiritual Well-Being
By Steven A. Rapp. Foreword by Tamar Frankiel, PhD and Judy Greenfeld. Preface by Hart Lazer.
7 x 10, 128 pp, b/w photos, Quality PB, Layflat binding, 978-1-58023-162-6 **$16.95**

Entering the Temple of Dreams: Jewish Prayers, Movements, and Meditations for the End of the Day *By Tamar Frankiel, PhD, and Judy Greenfeld*
7 x 10, 192 pp, illus., Quality PB, 978-1-58023-079-7 **$16.95**

Does the Soul Survive? A Jewish Journey to Belief in Afterlife, Past Lives & Living with Purpose *By Rabbi Elie Kaplan Spitz; Foreword by Brian L Weiss, MD*
6 x 9, 288 pp, Quality PB, 978-1-58023-165-7 **$16.99**

First Steps to a New Jewish Spirit: Reb Zalman's Guide to Recapturing the Intimacy & Ecstasy in Your Relationship with God *By Rabbi Zalman M. Schachter-Shalomi with Donald Gropman* 6 x 9, 144 pp, Quality PB, 978-1-58023-182-4 **$16.95**

God in Our Relationships: Spirituality between People from the Teachings of Martin Buber *By Rabbi Dennis S. Ross* 5½ x 8½, 160 pp, Quality PB, 978-1-58023-147-3 **$16.95**

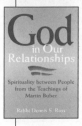

Judaism, Physics and God: Searching for Sacred Metaphors in a Post-Einstein World
By Rabbi David W. Nelson 6 x 9, 368 pp, Quality PB, inc. reader's discussion guide, 978-1-58023-306-4 **$18.99**;
HC, 352 pp, 978-1-58023-252-4 **$24.99**

The Jewish Lights Spirituality Handbook: A Guide to Understanding, Exploring & Living a Spiritual Life *Edited by Stuart M. Matlins*
What exactly is "Jewish" about spirituality? How do I make it a part of my life? Fifty of today's foremost spiritual leaders share their ideas and experience with us.
6 x 9, 456 pp, Quality PB, 978-1-58023-093-3 **$19.99**

Bringing the Psalms to Life: How to Understand and Use the Book of Psalms
By Daniel F. Polish 6 x 9, 208 pp, Quality PB, 978-1-58023-157-2 **$16.95**;
HC, 978-1-58023-077-3 **$21.95**

God & the Big Bang: Discovering Harmony between Science & Spirituality
By Daniel C. Matt 6 x 9, 216 pp, Quality PB, 978-1-879045-89-7 **$16.99**

Minding the Temple of the Soul: Balancing Body, Mind, and Spirit through Traditional Jewish Prayer, Movement, and Meditation *By Tamar Frankiel, PhD, and Judy Greenfeld*
7 x 10, 184 pp, illus., Quality PB, 978-1-879045-64-4 **$16.95**
Audiotape of the Blessings and Meditations: 60 min. **$9.95**
Videotape of the Movements and Meditations: 46 min. **$20.00**

One God Clapping: The Spiritual Path of a Zen Rabbi *By Alan Lew with Sherril Jaffe*
5½ x 8½, 336 pp, Quality PB, 978-1-58023-115-2 **$16.95**

There Is No Messiah ... and You're It: The Stunning Transformation of Judaism's Most Provocative Idea *By Rabbi Robert N. Levine, DD*
6 x 9, 192 pp, Quality PB, 978-1-58023-255-5 **$16.99**

These Are the Words: A Vocabulary of Jewish Spiritual Life
By Arthur Green 6 x 9, 304 pp, Quality PB, 978-1-58023-107-7 **$18.95**

Inspiration

God's To-Do List: 103 Ways to Be an Angel and Do God's Work on Earth
By Dr. Ron Wolfson 6 x 9, 150 pp, Quality PB, 978-1-58023-301-9 **$15.99**

God in All Moments: Mystical & Practical Spiritual Wisdom from Hasidic Masters
Edited and translated by Or N. Rose with Ebn D. Leader
5½ x 8½, 192 pp, Quality PB, 978-1-58023-186-2 **$16.95**

Our Dance with God: Finding Prayer, Perspective and Meaning in the Stories of Our
Lives *By Karyn D. Kedar* 6 x 9, 176 pp, Quality PB, 978-1-58023-202-9 **$16.99**

Also Available: **The Dance of the Dolphin** (HC edition of *Our Dance with God*)
6 x 9, 176 pp, HC, 978-1-58023-154-1 **$19.95**

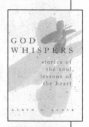

The Empty Chair: Finding Hope and Joy—Timeless Wisdom from a Hasidic Master,
Rebbe Nachman of Breslov *Adapted by Moshe Mykoff and the Breslov Research Institute*
4 x 6, 128 pp, 2-color text, Deluxe PB w/flaps, 978-1-879045-67-5 **$9.95**

The Gentle Weapon: Prayers for Everyday and Not-So-Everyday Moments—
Timeless Wisdom from the Teachings of the Hasidic Master, Rebbe Nachman of Breslov
Adapted by Moshe Mykoff and S. C. Mizrahi, together with the Breslov Research Institute
4 x 6, 144 pp, 2-color text, Deluxe PB w/flaps, 978-1-58023-022-3 **$9.99**

God Whispers: Stories of the Soul, Lessons of the Heart *By Karyn D. Kedar*
6 x 9, 176 pp, Quality PB, 978-1-58023-088-9 **$15.95**

An Orphan in History: One Man's Triumphant Search for His Jewish Roots
By Paul Cowan; Afterword by Rachel Cowan. 6 x 9, 288 pp, Quality PB, 978-1-58023-135-0 **$16.95**

Restful Reflections: Nighttime Inspiration to Calm the Soul, Based on Jewish Wisdom
By Rabbi Kerry M. Olitzky & Rabbi Lori Forman 4½ x 6¼, 448 pp, Quality PB, 978-1-58023-091-9 **$15.95**

Sacred Intentions: Daily Inspiration to Strengthen the Spirit, Based on Jewish Wisdom
By Rabbi Kerry M. Olitzky and Rabbi Lori Forman 4½ x 6¼, 448 pp, Quality PB, 978-1-58023-061-2 **$15.95**

Kabbalah/Mysticism/Enneagram

Awakening to Kabbalah: The Guiding Light of Spiritual Fulfillment
By Rav Michael Laitman, PhD 6 x 9, 192 pp, HC, 978-1-58023-264-7 **$21.99**

Seek My Face: A Jewish Mystical Theology *By Arthur Green*
6 x 9, 304 pp, Quality PB, 978-1-58023-130-5 **$19.95**

Zohar: Annotated & Explained
Translation and annotation by Daniel C. Matt; Foreword by Andrew Harvey
5½ x 8½, 176 pp, Quality PB, 978-1-893361-51-5 **$15.99** *(A SkyLight Paths book)*

Cast in God's Image: Discover Your Personality Type Using the Enneagram and Kabbalah
By Rabbi Howard A. Addison
7 x 9, 176 pp, Quality PB, Layflat binding, 20+ journaling exercises, 978-1-58023-124-4 **$16.95**

Ehyeh: A Kabbalah for Tomorrow
By Arthur Green 6 x 9, 224 pp, Quality PB, 978-1-58023-213-5 **$16.99**

The Enneagram and Kabbalah, 2nd Edition: Reading Your Soul
By Rabbi Howard A. Addison 6 x 9, 192 pp, Quality PB, 978-1-58023-229-6 **$16.99**

Finding Joy: A Practical Spiritual Guide to Happiness *By Dannel I. Schwartz with Mark Hass*
6 x 9, 192 pp, Quality PB, 978-1-58023-009-4 **$14.95**

The Flame of the Heart: Prayers of a Chasidic Mystic *By Reb Noson of Breslov. Translated by
David Sears with the Breslov Research Institute* 5 x 7¼, 160 pp, Quality PB, 978-1-58023-246-3 **$15.99**

The Gift of Kabbalah: Discovering the Secrets of Heaven, Renewing Your Life on Earth
By Tamar Frankiel, PhD 6 x 9, 256 pp, Quality PB, 978-1-58023-141-1 **$16.95;**
HC, 978-1-58023-108-4 **$21.95**

Kabbalah: A Brief Introduction for Christians
By Tamar Frankiel, PhD 5½ x 8½, 208 pp, Quality PB, 978-1-58023-303-3 **$16.99**

The Lost Princess and Other Kabbalistic Tales of Rebbe Nachman of Breslov
The Seven Beggars and Other Kabbalistic Tales of Rebbe Nachman of Breslov
Translated by Rabbi Aryeh Kaplan; Preface by Rabbi Chaim Kramer
Lost Princess: 6 x 9, 400 pp, Quality PB, 978-1-58023-217-3 **$18.99**
Seven Beggars: 6 x 9, 192 pp, Quality PB, 978-1-58023-250-0 **$16.99**

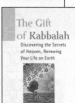

See also *The Way Into Jewish Mystical Tradition* in Spirituality / Lawrence Kushner

About Jewish Lights

People of all faiths and backgrounds yearn for books that attract, engage, educate, and spiritually inspire.

Our principal goal is to stimulate thought and help all people learn about who the Jewish People are, where they come from, and what the future can be made to hold. While people of our diverse Jewish heritage are the primary audience, our books speak to people in the Christian world as well and will broaden their understanding of Judaism and the roots of their own faith.

We bring to you authors who are at the forefront of spiritual thought and experience. While each has something different to say, they all say it in a voice that you can hear.

Our books are designed to welcome you and then to engage, stimulate, and inspire. We judge our success not only by whether or not our books are beautiful and commercially successful, but by whether or not they make a difference in your life.

For your information and convenience, at the back of this book we have provided a list of other Jewish Lights books you might find interesting and useful. They cover all the categories of your life:

Bar/Bat Mitzvah	Life Cycle
Bible Study / Midrash	Meditation
Children's Books	Parenting
Congregation Resources	Prayer
Current Events / History	Ritual / Sacred Practice
Ecology	Spirituality
Fiction: Mystery, Science Fiction	Theology / Philosophy
Grief / Healing	Travel
Holidays / Holy Days	12-Step
Inspiration	Women's Interest
Kabbalah / Mysticism / Enneagram	

Stuart M. Matlins, Publisher

Or phone, fax, mail or e-mail to: **JEWISH LIGHTS Publishing**
Sunset Farm Offices, Route 4 • P.O. Box 237 • Woodstock, Vermont 05091
Tel: (802) 457-4000 • Fax: (802) 457-4004 • www.jewishlights.com
Credit card orders: (800) 962-4544 (8:30AM–5:30PM ET Monday–Friday)
Generous discounts on quantity orders. SATISFACTION GUARANTEED. Prices subject to change.

For more information about each book, visit our website at www.jewishlights.com